SELF-ASSESSMENT AND DEVELOPMENT IN WRITING

A COLLABORATIVE INQUIRY

WRITTEN LANGUAGE
S E R I E S

Marcia Farr, senior editor

SELF-ASSESSMENT AND DEVELOPMENT IN WRITING

A COLLABORATIVE INQUIRY

edited by

Jane Bowman Smith
Winthrop University

Kathleen Blake Yancey
Clemson University

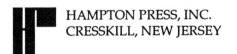
HAMPTON PRESS, INC.
CRESSKILL, NEW JERSEY

Printed in the United States of America

Library of Congress Cataloging-in-Publication Data

Self-assessment and development in writing : a collaborative inquiry / edited by Jane Bowman Smith and Kathleen Blake Yancey
    p. cm. -- (Written language series)
Includes bibliographic references and indexes.
ISBN 1-58283-146-X -- ISBN 1-57273-147-8 (pbk.)
  1. English language--Rhetoric--Study and teaching. 2. Report writing--Study and teaching. 3. Students--self rating of. I. Smith, Jane Bowman. II. Yancey, Kathleen Blake, 1950- III. Series.

PE1404.S37 1999
808'042'07--dc21

                                     99-050312

Hampton Press, Inc.
23 Broadway
Cresskill, NJ 07626

To Frederik, Kirsten, my father,
and the memory of my dear mother

To my three best friends:
David, Genevieve, and Matthew

CONTENTS

PREFACE

As more than a few people have noted, Composition Studies has a bad habit of forgetting what's valuable. Or, to put it another way, we sometimes seem to move from one key idea to the next (or is it one fashion to the next?) without fully exploring what we might learn from each idea. To cite two well known examples, enthusiasm for composing process theory and research seems largely replaced by devotion to cultural studies, and while basic writers haven't disappeared, the attention given to them has waned considerably.

Self-assessment, of course, is among the topics in composition and rhetoric that in earlier days appeared to offer some luster, then to lose it. As Tom Hilgers, Edna Hussey, and Monica Stitt-Bergh outline it in the first chapter of this volume, the history of self-assessment is closely linked to research on composing, and specifically to the kinds of judgments writers make in the process of composing and to the effects of those judgments in forming a writer. Given the absence of interest in composing processes, then, it might seem a bit of a surprise that we're offering this volume on self-assessment. After all, postmodernism hasn't come under erasure, nor has *process* suddenly become particularly compelling.

We think otherwise, as you might well imagine. During the last ten years, a convergence of concerns has forwarded the role that self-assessment plays in many kinds of teaching and learning behaviors. For instance, the teaching portfolio used for both employment and promotion, as well as for learning itself, is predicated on the idea that a practicing teacher can discern what works and what doesn't—that is, on self-assessment. Similarly, with their reflective texts, writing portfolios have foregrounded the role that self-assessment plays in writer development by asking that writers *make visible* the processes that before, only researchers studied. And as we have recently seen in placement assessments in several places—among them Coe College and Grand Valley State University—self assessment provides another way of locating students appropriately, by tapping the self-assessments they have already engaged in, at least tacitly.

Collectively, the contents of this volume address all these concerns while they do something else: take on the questions about agency embedded in self-assessment that are posed by postmodernism. A particular value of the volume, then, is that it carries forward previous pedagogical and research work at the same time that it addresses the theoretical issues threatening to undermine self-assessment. More specifically, it does this by understanding *self* assessment as a phenomenon that can be approached in several ways.

- Most obvious of these approaches, perhaps, is through our experiences in the classroom—and contributors here, from Sam Watson to Jane Smith and Vicki Collins, do just that: they come to the topic as teachers, discussing how self-assessment helps students learn better. It seems a "natural" route to take.
- Another "natural" route is that provided by Rebecca Howard. The *program* she describes may well have been the first to use self-assessment as a placement vehicle.
- Chris Anson and Hilgers and company look at the rhetorical situation of writing and response. Anson connects self-assessment with his interest in response to student writing. Tom Hilgers et al. locate their interest in self-assessment with research on how self-monitoring can alter behavior, a concern that also located Hilgers' dissertation.
- Janice Lauer and Susan Latta bring a feminist perspective to a postmodern analysis of self-assessment.
- Previously an editor of *College Composition and Communication*, Richard Larson—not surprisingly, perhaps—sees self-assessment through the lens of careful reading and editorial work.
- And two contributors here bring their experiences as faculty developers to self-assessment, Irwin Weiser to talk about how we can nurture a capacity for self-assessment in our newest colleagues, Sandra Mano to reflect on how the growth attributed to self-assessment can sometimes offer discomfort as well as insight.
- Finally, the editors of the volume bring together the concerns that cut across and beyond the chapters, concerns about agency, of

course, about efficacy, about ways to weave self-assessment into learning environments, and learning with and from our students about the impact of such weaving. We also raise questions that we hope any new work on self-assessment will take up and take forward.

* * * * *

The logic of this volume's arrangement also merits comment. The first chapter provides a context for self-assessment in its historicizing of the phenomenon: it brings together research in composition studies and psychology to suggest both what we know and how we might work. Accordingly, it provides an introduction to the volume itself. The second chapter, by Susan Latta and Janice Lauer, talks back to the first as it takes up some of the challenges to self-assessment that current theory poses, finally deciding that agency is possible after all. Rebecca Howard also sounds theoretical concerns while moving to the practical and ethical issues of placement assessment. And Chris Anson concludes this conceptual section of the volume in offering a research model on response and self-assessment that is grounded in and recommends practice.

The classroom itself is the locus of the next several chapters. Sam Watson defines his reflective classroom, a place with self-assessment at its heart. Richard Larson also takes up how students might work, identifying the textual structures that make for the most effective self-assessment. Vicki Collins discusses how using self-assessment, not at the end of the writing process but in the middle, helps students identify past patterns of useful practice that can help them through the difficult transition from gathering data to synthesizing and drafting. Jane Smith then discusses how both teachers and students profit from students' self-assessments of their reading response journals.

The next conceptual section includes two chapters on faculty development: who is to help new teachers use self-assessment in the classroom? Irwin Weiser explains a technique that introduces new teachers to ways of reviewing and knowing their own practice so as to enhance it. And Sandra Mano explores, in a painful moment of self-assessment, why faculty development efforts, despite the insights they offer, don't always work.

The final chapter, then, brings together these perspectives to define self-assessment as presented here, to show the connections among the chapters as well as the disjunctions, and to suggest the kinds of questions to which we need answers.

* * * * *

This volume on self-assessment has been years in the making. In the time that the collection has developed, self-assessment has emerged as a topic—connected as it is to writing process, cognition, reflection, and college course placement—that indeed warrants its own examination.

Which makes this volume more timely than ever.

Kathleen Blake Yancey and Jane Bowman Smith
1999

SERIES PREFACE

This series examines the characteristics of *writing* in the human world. Volumes in the series present scholarly work on written language in its various contexts. Across time and space, human beings use various forms of written language—or writing systems—to fulfill a range of social, cultural, and personal functions, and this diversity can be studies from a variety of perspectives within both the social sciences and the humanities, including those of linguistics, anthropology, psychology, education, rhetoric, literacy criticism, philosophy, and history. Although writing is not often used apart from oral language, or without aspects of reading, and thus many volumes in this series include other facets of language and communication, writing itself receives primary emphasis.

This volume examines the critical notion of self-assessment from a plurality of viewpoints. It offers history, current theory, and ethical issues, as well as a research model grounded in practice. Such a conceptual framework contextualizes the notion of self-assessment. The volume also shows how self-assessment in the classroom helps students learn better. A discussion of faculty development—specifically, how to nurture new colleagues and deal with discomfiture—is included. What is distinctive is how the editors weave together concerns that cut above and beyond the chapters. Thus, self-assessment is both made more reflexive and turned outward to future questions for new work.

While the study of writing is absorbing in its own right, it is an increasingly important social issue as well, as demographic movements occur around the world and as language and ethnicity accrue more intensely political meanings. Writing, and literacy more generally, is central to education, and education in turn is central to occupational and social mobility. Manuscripts that present either the results of empirical research, both qualitative and quantitative, or theoretical treatments of relevant issues are encouraged for submission.

ACKNOWLEDGMENTS

Many people have contributed to this volume. We would like to thank the friends and colleagues who listened to us patiently, sometimes offered advice, and sometimes wisely held their tongues; we would particularly like to thank our families, who believed in this project from its very beginnings, supported our efforts, and encouraged us—even when "the book" stubbornly demanded center stage.

Our contributors not only wrote sound and insightful essays from a wide range of perspectives but also served to inspire us; their belief in this project reinforced our own. Finally, we would like to thank the editorial staff of Hampton Press, Inc., who were enthusiastic about the project and accessible throughout the process of preparing the manuscript for publication, and particularly Barbara Bernstein, with whom it has been a pleasure to work: she combines professionalism with a lively optimism, an unbeatable combination.

We couldn't have done it without you.

1 THE CASE FOR PROMPTED SELF-ASSESSMENT IN THE WRITING CLASSROOM

Thomas L. Hilgers, Edna L. Hussey and Monica Stitt-Bergh

University of Hawai'i-Manoa

Everyone engages in self-assessment, often without being conscious of the processes. However, in certain communities, self-assessment is a conscious activity, actively taught and promoted. We start this chapter by touring a couple of these communities.

Our first stop: Total Fitness Center. The first thing we note is a bodybuilder sitting on a bench before sets of free weights, recording on a training schedule the pounds he has just hefted and the number of times he hefted them. Our tour guide then takes us over to the training room adjacent to the pool. There we observe an Olympic hopeful watching the tape of her dive—for the fifth time—in slow motion. We climb stairs to another viewing room where the quarterback of the local football team is studying and restudying the tape of several plays from the team's Saturday-night game with the Cougars.

We make our next stop at the Center for Arts Education. In the dance studios, we watch dancers observing themselves in mirrors, monitoring the heights of their lifts and the steadiness of their stances. Across the hall, in a room behind a stage, we find actors preparing *The Taming of the Shrew* by watching and critiquing a video of yesterday's rehearsal—with lots of hoots and hollers. Down a hall in what appears to be a lab, three actors discuss the gyrations on an oscilloscope as they listen to recordings of their individual renditions of Hamlet's first soliloquy.

We now make a final stop in a familiar scene: a writing classroom. Because many groups and individuals are at work, it takes us

1

a while to find our peer, the teacher. Finally Monica spots her, and we move over to listen in on what she is doing.

> *Teacher*: I want to listen to what you have written. Please read it to me.
> *Student*: "According to psychologist Rollo May . . . [student reads aloud her draft to the teacher] . . . in this age of anxiety." Oh, that's not making sense, is it?
> *Teacher*: [nods noncommittally.]
> *Student*: I'm going to have to fix that [takes a pencil and makes a note in the margin]. Right?
> *Teacher*: [nods noncommittally.]
> *Student*: "In contrast, Victor Frankl holds that . . ." [student continues to read] Oh, oh. It contradicts what I said up there, right?
> *Teacher*: [nods noncommittally.]

We nod to one another, acknowledging the way our colleague is using Donald Murray's "silent" approach to conferencing.

When we get back home, we pause to reflect on our brief tour and on the versions of self-assessment we observed. Very few of us would readily link the worlds of sports and performance with writing classrooms. However, in each of those worlds we saw students intent on reflection-in-action (Schön, 1987), a process of thinking back on an action, recognizing an error or unexpected result, acting on this recognition, and then adjusting behavior to improve proficiency.

Clearly, a practice as frequent and widespread as self-assessment must have significant utility. Why, then, has self-assessment received so little attention in recent scholarship on writing? Before we propose two reasons for what has to be more than an oversight, we present a critical review of literature on self-assessment—primarily grounded in social and clinical psychology—in an effort to identify components of the self-assessment enterprise that may be particularly significant to writers and writing teachers. After identifying key aspects of self-assessment, we shift to the research on writing and self-assessment. Finally, we review and propose approaches to the teaching of self-assessment that might move it into the mainstream of writing teachers' strategies.

SELF-ASSESSMENT IN SOCIAL AND CLINICAL PSYCHOLOGY

"In the beginning"—not of time, but of contemporary self-assessment studies—the parent of self-evaluation, called *self-observation* or *self-*

monitoring, was regarded primarily as a tool for gathering observational data. However, it did not take long before studies began to report that self-observation by itself was leading to behavior change (Kanfer & Phillips, 1966). Scores of studies, including many with such practical goals as helping a person quit smoking or lose weight, were conducted on the effects of self-monitoring techniques. This was an interesting switch. For a long time in psychological research, self-observation had been considered an obstacle to the study of behavior. Everyone knew that when people are conscious of what they are doing, they react to watching themselves; they are not behaving "normally." The applied research on self-observation turned the tables and made this so-called reactivity factor, at least when it involved something like smoking, into an agency of desired behavior change. Indeed, by the late 1960s some psychologists were proclaiming that guided self-assessment techniques might obviate an individual's need for more traditional approaches to therapy (Tharp & Wetzel, 1969). By 1974 the literature on self-observation was so extensive that it needed to be brought together in a review article (Kazdin, 1974).

Although the word *evaluation* occasionally appeared in discussions, the formal behaviorist paradigm of the period did not specifically include an assessment component under the rubric *self-observation*. *Self-monitoring*, for example, formally involved only the systematic observation and recording of one's own behavior. There were clear parameters for what was to be observed, when it was to be observed, and how the recording of observations would take place. Thus, a person might note either the commencement of an activity or an urge; the recording, often by pencil on paper, might occur immediately after the activity or at a recurring interval. Several studies (e.g., Johnson & White, 1971; Mahoney, Moore, Wade, & Moura, 1973; McFall, 1970) demonstrated that such antiseptic behavior, not including an evaluative component, affected subsequent behavior, often dramatically. However, effects were not uniform. When Kazdin (1974) reviewed studies that involved self-monitoring, he found that the therapeutic effects of self-monitoring appeared to attenuate across time. Interestingly, he also found that when effects occurred, they were not particularly dependent on either the accuracy or the reliability of a subject's observation of the behavior.

Results from several studies suggested that it was not self-monitoring alone that was the agent for behavior change. Some suggested that the *personal value*, or *valence*, assigned a particular behavior played a large role in shaping any behavior change associated with self-monitoring. Thus, for example, self-observation of eating behavior was likely to result in less eating if a plump person valued appearing slender, but not if the person attached no particular value to slender appearance.

A second key, but not carefully studied, component in studies on self-monitoring was *motivation*. McFall and Hammen (1971) cited motivation to change as one of three treatment factors most likely responsible for behavior change. Even in studies where a motivational component was not in any way controlled, motivation to change usually seemed presumed. The importance of motivation was to some extent borne out in results reported by Lipinski, Black, Nelson, and Ciminero (1975), who found that subjects in a self-monitoring experiment who were motivated to stop smoking smoked significantly less during the 4-week study than did students who had enrolled not because they wanted to quit smoking, but because they were smokers. In her review of the literature, Kopp (1988) found that behavior changed whether the subjects were motivated or not. However, she suggested that long-term maintenance of the new behavior was more likely when the person is motivated. Finally, we should also note that valence and motivation are often confounded and cannot be measured independently.

Finally, the *frequency* of self-assessment is another possible factor influencing reactivity. Frequent monitoring led to more continuous awareness and allowed more opportunities to self-reward. However, self-monitoring that is tedious and time-consuming can be too distracting and lead ultimately to ineffective self-monitoring (Bornstein, Hamilton, & Bornstein, 1986). Studies also found that reinforcement, including self-reinforcement, generally enhanced the effects of self-monitoring (Connell & Carta, 1993).

In sum, studies have reported that self-observation can change many kinds of behavior: smoking, eating, studying, face touching, and cleaning up of living space. Effects were often enhanced through coupling self-observation with reinforcement and external therapy. In reviewing studies that involved self-monitoring without reinforcement, Zimmerman and Levitt (1975) found a pattern of effects: Self-monitoring with a wrist counter alone produced no effect with 27% of the cases; an increase in "knowledge, awareness, and understanding" in 36% of the cases; behavior change plus increase in "knowledge" and so forth in 27%; and behavior change with no reported increase in "knowledge" in 9% of the cases. In reviewing studies that included reinforcement and/or training, Bornstein et al. (1986) reported that accuracy is enhanced when immediate feedback regarding accuracy is provided. Training and supervised practice are also deemed necessary for accurate self-monitoring. Finally, the effects of self-observation were found to vary by task: Smoking typically decreased (Fredericksen, Epstein, & Kosevsky, 1975), whereas "ecological acts" (riding a bicycle, returning bottles to a grocery store) did not change in frequency (Hoon, 1976). Such differences were often presumed to be a function of valence. Other studies suggested that self-observation, even when unreliable (Cavior & Marabott, 1976), has at least as much effect on behavior as does a person's knowledge of being externally observed.

Models That Explain the Effects of Self-Observation and Self-Assessment

Why does self-monitoring affect behavior? Most studies from the 1970s explained the effect by pointing to Kanfer's (1975) "feedback loop." The Kanfer Model says basically this: Self-monitoring provides an individual with feedback that allows the individual to discriminate between his or her current level of behavior and some significant social or individual standard. This discrimination leads the individual to reward or punish him- or herself at each future self-monitored occurrence.

This model is important in that it suggests an evaluation component to be central to the mechanism of behavior change. The key to behavior change, if Kanfer was correct, is the discrimination between present performance and a significant standard. Nelson, Lipinski, and Black (1976) claimed support for Kanfer's model from the simple fact that changes resulting from self-monitoring are generally in the desired therapeutic direction. Kazdin (1974) indicated the important, although not altogether indispensable, role played by specifying performance standards in achieving maximum effects; however, Kazdin also reported that self-monitoring can have effects even when subjects do not have access to feedback from their observations. Studies by Richards and his colleagues (Richards, McReynolds, Holt, & Sexton, 1976a; Richards, Perri, & Gortney, 1976b) found no significant differences associated with degree of specificity of feedback.

Another model of self-assessment effects may be important to what we say below about self-assessment and writers. This model, supported in studies by Cavior and Marabott (1976) and Bellack, Rozensky, and Schwartz (1974), holds that the power of self-assessment derives in part from the way it interrupts stereotypic behavior change. In other words, the very act of observing—or observing plus recording, or observing and evaluating—interrupts stereotypic "autopilot" behavior. If new stimuli of the moment achieve some dominance, subsequent behavior is more likely to be in response to the new stimuli than a resumption of an "autopilot" chain of behaviors.

From the Behaviorist Perspective: Key Components of Self-Assessment

In sum, the foregoing review of studies leads us to focus on several aspects of self-assessment that are likely to be keys in determining its utility in particular circumstances. The most robust among findings in research on self-monitoring and self-assessment lead us to posit that *self-assessment is likely to promote positive effects in situations where*:

- *Self-assessment is engaged in systematically.* Frequent, regular, and integrated self-assessments can be predicted to affect the learner's subsequent behavior and knowledge.
- *Self-assessment processes are embedded in a "facilitating" context that pays attention to the need for incentives, personal involvement, rewards, and training.* The direction, intensity, and duration of the behavior change related to self-monitoring are likely to be affected by the learner's motivation; the personal value of the behavior to the learner; internal or external reinforcements associated with changed behavior; and the learner's fluency (through training and practice) with the processes of self-monitoring.
- *The approach to self-assessment provides, or prompts the generation of, appropriate criteria, and offers some guidance in the application of those criteria.* Several studies suggest that the standards or criteria used in the assessment are key determinants of whether or not subsequent behavior will be "improved" or "more successful."
- *The approach breaks complex assessment tasks into manageable units and helps learners to apply clear criteria when they deal with the content of a particular unit.* Self-assessment seems most helpful in improving a given behavior when that behavior is related to performance standards that are clear, simple, and easy benchmarks for evaluation.
- *The approach ensures that "typical behavior" will be interrupted at points where assessment is most likely to make a difference.* A primary function of self-assessment is to interrupt a chain of stereotypic behavior. The very act of interruption allows new stimuli an opportunity to come to the attention of the self-assessor. To the extent that the stimuli are seen by the self-assessor as pointing in desirable directions, the stimuli are likely to guide both new learning and effective decision making.

SELF-ASSESSMENT IN COMPOSITION STUDIES:
A PROMISE NOT FULFILLED

As noted in the literature review earlier, self-observation was one of the more prominent areas of social science research in the 1960s and 1970s. In the 1980s, however, many of the studies were regarded as dusty, if not downright forgettable. Research fashions were changing. The behaviorist revolution in American psychology was on its last legs. Cognitivism was on the rise. Studies of self-observation were being replaced by studies of problem-solving strategies and their effects.

It was during this period that the Flower and Hayes (1981a) model of the composing process became dominant in composition studies and that research on evaluation took center stage. According to the model, revision is embedded in the "reviewing" process, and actual modifications of strategy or text are the results of evaluations. The "monitor," which functions constantly, is moment by moment implicitly making evaluations of the writer's current course of activity. The model was often cited in, and was sometimes directly responsible for, the myriad of studies of composing processes produced during the "miracle decade" of composition studies.

Because the Flower and Hayes model mentioned a cognitive "monitor," it spawned a number of studies of writers' self-assessments. Some of Flower's (1979) own research looked particularly closely at assessment functions, as did a few other studies. Bridwell (1980), Emig (1971), Nold (1980), and Sommers (1980), among others, described evaluations that resulted in authors' making changes to their text. Evaluation acts occur frequently, even with children (e.g., Bissex, 1980; Dyson, 1983). However, few studies focused primarily on actual evaluation acts. Miller (1982) and Sommers (1980) considered the standards for evaluation that writers used and found that some conventional standards (e.g., coherence, aesthetic appeal) were seldom mentioned by professionals. Beach (1976) noted that college students' evaluations were frequently unrelated to real problems in their texts, but rather mimicked textbook evaluations. Newkirk (1982) and Hilgers (1984) reported that beginning writers' evaluations often derived from experiences and considerations outside of a particular text. Hilgers (1986) demonstrated the tenacity of nontextual standards in a study that looked at young writers across 3 years of development.

As it turned out, however, these studies did not constitute a critical mass. What did catch on was the methodology used by Flower and Hayes (1981b) in the development of their cognitive model: analysis of the think-aloud "protocols" of writers at work. In fact, "protocol analysis" became synonymous with cognitive studies of composition.

When we look at the quick rise to dominance of social constructivist theory in the 1990s, it may appear that cognitivism, like behaviorism, has become unfashionable. It may appear that "changing fashions" are keeping attention from self-assessment. Actually, however, the rise of social constructivist theory was not just a matter of changing hemlines and silhouettes. To a large extent, social constructivism evolved as a criticism of cognitivists' lack of attention to the social contexts within which writers function.

Social constructivist theory makes clear that all behavior, including "individual" behavior, is influenced by the social contexts in which it was learned or is performed (see Berlin, 1987; Bruffee, 1984). This points to a core problem with the notion of self-assessment. Most of the work on self-assessment reviewed here earlier, whether done under the label of "self-observation" or "cognitive monitor functions," attempted to view self-assessment essentially as a set of isolated acts. It did not explicitly recognize the social situations in which individuals learned the strategies of self-assessment and, just as importantly, the socially contextualized criteria that individuals used in making their assessments. As a result, both the behaviorist and cognitivist approaches to the study of self-assessment were extremely limited in pointing to ways in which an individual's self-assessments could be made more effective, and thus lead an individual to become a better writer.

The lack of focus on how we learn self-assessment leads us to what we propose as the second reason for the lack of attention to self-assessment in scholarship on writing. That reason is this: A writer's self-assessments are often idiosyncratic and, in the view of readers, frequently inaccurate. Further, self-assessment, even if accurate, does not in and of itself point the way to effective action.

Even if we assert that an author is self-assessing virtually all of the time (Hilgers, 1984), we have to accept that the act of self-assessment means very little unless it prompts appropriate consequent action. Consider for a moment a common self-assessment behavior: looking in the mirror. For most of us, virtually every visit to a restroom includes one or more glances in the mirror. However, we do not just glance into the mirror because we value the self-assessment associated with looking in the mirror. No, we look into the mirror to decide if we look the way we want to look. We look into the mirror to inform a decision on whether to recomb our hair, straighten our tie, adjust our collar, remove lint from a blouse, or freshen our makeup. We do not stop simply with the act of self-assessment. We decide whether action should follow and, if further action is necessary, which of several possible courses to take. To use self-assessment effectively, writers need to follow similar processes. However, there is little in the existing formal research on self-assessment to suggest how a writer might choose a profitable course after making a self-assessment.

THE PROMISE OF RESEARCH-GUIDED PRACTICES IN THE CLASSROOM

When we move from research on self-assessment to a consideration of research-guided practices for writing classrooms, we find both possibilities and potential problems. Certain commentaries emphasize the value of self-assessment practices (Beach, 1976, 1982; Beach & Anson, 1988; Beach & Eaton, 1984; Flower, Hayes, Carey, Shriver, & Stratman, 1986; White, 1994, 1995). Advocates have suggested assessment processes and methods by which communities of teachers and students can observe writers' self-competence and development (Badger, Dilena, Peters, Webster, & Weeks, 1991; Herman, Aschbacher, & Winters, 1992). In addition, narratives of self-assessment practices by Graves (1983), Hansen, Newkirk, and Graves (1985), Calkins (1986), Rief (1991), and Atwell (1987) suggest sensible, useful paths toward a better writing pedagogy. A growing body of teacher researchers (Cochran-Smith & Lytle, 1993; Daiker & Morenberg, 1990; Goswami & Stillman, 1987) have documented their efforts to define and study assessment issues at the classroom level. Currently the National Writing Project and other teacher-research communities are organizing the collective body of classroom research so that it is accessible to all teachers.

However, when we look at random classrooms—at least here in Hawai'i—we see problems. Teachers embrace the theoretical promise of self-assessment, although few devote much time to its practice. Why? We find a number of obstacles: a lack of teacher training in the uses of self-assessment and a lack of understanding of its links with curriculum and instruction; "content-driven" demands on instructional time; and a lack of evidence beyond personal testimony of its benefits (Hussey, Bayer, Hilgers, & Jones, 1995). Despite these obstacles, there are pockets of extensive use, especially among the population of teachers nationwide who as elementary classroom teachers are familiar with the practices of holistic education, whole language learning, and student-centered classrooms. In such classrooms, practices are based on the principle that students grow and learn most effectively when they are actively engaged in their own learning (Weaver, 1990)—and that requires self-assessment, reflection on its results, and consequent attempts at different practices.

The rest of this chapter is a reflection on particular practices that the authors find to hold the most promise of bringing effective self-assessment into the forefront of writers' (and teachers') strategies. We begin by proposing a template of questions that teachers can ask when they consider or plan new writing activities for their students and then describe several activities that meet some or even most of the criteria set by the template.

ACTIVITIES FOR HELPING WRITERS TO LEARN EFFECTIVE SELF-ASSESSMENT

The research we reviewed earlier, social-constructivist theory, and our own experience lead us now to propose eight questions that, if when asked of a certain set of activities can be answered "yes," are likely to prompt effective learning. The questions are:

1. Does the approach to instruction integrate self-monitoring and assessment systematically into a writer's strategies?
2. Does the approach use the social context of the classroom in ways that encourage the writer to attach personal value to what he or she is writing and help motivate the writer to improve?
3. Does the approach use the social contexts of students as frames for discussions of standards and assessment criteria?
4. Does the approach help students make connections between standards, self-assessments, and strategies for further drafting or revising?
5. Does the approach break up the rhetorical situation into parts that allow the application of relatively clear and discrete evaluation standards for different situations?
6. Does each act of self-assessment increase the writer's awareness of a variety of alternative strategies that may be more effective than the stereotypic strategy?
7. Does the approach use self-assessment to interrupt well learned but less than optimally effective writing behavior chains?
8. Does the approach include training and practice in self-assessment techniques?

The activities to which we now turn grow out of our understanding of what makes self-assessment work effectively. Our enthusiasm for a particular activity is a reflection of the likelihood that the activity allows each of the eight questions to be answered with a "yes."

Helping Students Discover Useful Standards

How Students Learn Standards. Clear standards—of what constitutes good writing, effective revision, appropriate editing—will lead to better self-assessments. Students learn writing standards in a variety of ways, many of them not directly focused on criteria: through a teacher's description of an assignment and expectations; through class discussions about texts and what works and does not work; through discussions of how an assignment will be graded; and by way of teachers' interactions with students in conferences or through written feedback. In these domains, the "content" under consideration spans spectra of feedback: from ideas to mechanics; from directive (emphasis on textual errors) to facilitative (emphasis on procedures and strategies for particular purposes; Knoblauch & Brannon, 1984). The variety of criteria or standards can become embedded in the writer's "monitor" and can be called into play when the writer self-assesses.

Standards setting also occurs when students work with their own peers, as in writing groups or peer-feedback groups. Since 1980, Elbow has advocated the use of the peer audience as a "focusing force" and monitor for writing assessment. Ideally, students in feedback groups internalize their peers' comments into a self-assessment checklist or set of standards that undergoes periodic revision (see Bruffee, 1986).

Student writers, if asked, can articulate writing standards. Students in primary school cite feelings about subject matter as well as length and neatness when asked to judge their own writing (Hilgers, 1984, 1986). When we asked high school students and first-year college students to characterize "good writing" (Hussey et al., 1995), every student responded, and most offered traits such as "clear," "organized," "correct grammar, spelling, punctuation." When first-year college students were interviewed about their performance on final drafts assigned by instructors from different disciplines, students offered comments that focused primarily on grammatical correctness ("I didn't use any *is's* or *was's*") or on matters of form ("I wrote five pages like I was supposed to" or "I wrote a complete essay with an introduction, body, and conclusion").

Over time, any criteria that are sustained in classroom instruction evolve for students into fixed procedural rules—such as "All thesis statements should contain three distinct points and then be supported by examples in three paragraphs." Unfortunately, as students write and self-assess what they write, they tend to apply such rules to all writing situations indiscriminately, regardless of the particulars of a rhetorical context. Potentially more applicable standards—"good writing says something true and important, unique and powerful, something of substance that enriches the reader's experience" (Hawai'i Department of Education, 1994)—are unfortunately often fluffed off by students because they do not include rules for their accomplishment.

Hence, we begin to see why the articulation of standards, although necessary,will not alone provide adequate guidance to ensure the transformation of writing practices (LeMahieu & Foss, 1994). Standards need illustrations, contexts, and explanations of what they mean in terms of instructional practices. Student writers need to experience various and frequent self-assessment practices in order to work more independently at improving their own writing. We now consider some ways in which teachers work to engender effective standards for writers.

How Teachers "Teach" Standards. A common practice among teachers is to give an assignment to students with the assumption that their students already know what is expected of them. When students are unable to deliver, teachers are bewildered by students' apparent deficiencies. Perhaps a critical first step in promoting self-assessment, then, is to design writing assignments that include information about expectations. Class discussions on an instructor's overt and covert expectations can become a valuable opportunity for helping students develop real knowledge about self-assessment (Larson, 1971).

White (1994) at California State University contended that the design of writing assignments is in itself an aspect of assessment because we give students specific tasks, even prescribing form and content, then assess the ways in which students should have conformed to or extended assignments. He suggested that students should discuss a writing assignment extensively—its language, purposes, goals, and audience(s)—before drafting. After students submit their drafts, the instructor selects from that collection or from a previous collection some sample essays around which *students themselves derive a rubric* that is then used for assessment purposes. Students can also read examples of professional writing on the same topic, in the same genre, and apply to these samples the class-developed rubrics for evaluation. This strategy for setting standards differs from traditional practice where models of "good" writing are cursorily examined and then imitated without students' coming to a clear understanding of what makes the exemplar exemplary. In addition, if students provide one another feedback, within peer response groups, they can identify and categorize specific peer comments that may be later used to expand or refine class-generated standards.

The National Writing Project, devoted to concerns of teaching writing, has been successful at promoting similar self-assessment practices among its teacher consultants. Following the model of teachers teaching teachers, Writing Project teachers demonstrate a variety of self-assessment practices and meet periodically to discuss and refine strategies. Routman, a Writing Project consultant and resource teacher for elementary grades in Ohio, offered the practice of whole-class responses to teachers' questions as a way of articulating writing standards. For example, second graders in Ellen Rubin's class wrote their own pieces and then discussed what they had learned about what good writers do: "After they write a story, they read it over to see if it makes sense and it's the way they want it"; "They write with detail; they tell what happened" (Routman, 1991). Posting a class-generated list of standards built around students' responses helps students to internalize qualities of good writing so they learn to better self-assess their own writing. Teachers then encourage students to work toward one or two posted standards on the next assignment. Further, teachers can analyze student standards and use what they learn to inform their teaching or revise the curriculum.

Ways to Build Self-Assessment into a Writer's Processes

Portfolios, Postwrites, Postscripts. Another key to effective self-assessment is users' familiarity with the procedures of assessment. Providing sustained practice with assessing writing and making it central to teaching together help students develop habits of mind that become standard behavior inside and outside the writing classroom.

Building assessment activities around the compilation of writers' portfolios offers promise of developing such habits of mind. Despite a dearth of supporting research evidence, and despite conflicting concerns over reliability and validity, the use of portfolio assessment continues to grow in classrooms where educators have perceived the need to assess writing as both process and product. Teachers are claiming through their own classroom-based research that portfolios are effective instructional and evaluative tools, in part because of the self-assessment strategies that students learn as they construct their portfolios.

Having students choose pieces to place in (or remove from) a portfolio of "best writing" provides teachers with excellent opportunities to prompt the articulation of standards and to teach processes of self-assessment. However, the larger, pedagogically more significant, opportunity is presented prior to that selection: in the actual composition of pieces, specifically in whether and how students make explicit the reasons behind their choices of strategies as they write from drafts to final pieces.

Teachers often require students to submit self-assessment commentaries, sometimes called "postwrites" or "postscripts," with each of their portfolio pieces and a postwrite on their overall portfolio. Postwrites, or, generically, prompts for self-assessment, work toward building a habit of formative evaluation. Postwrites are often modeled as a defense of choices and require students to articulate the criteria they employed in their self-assessments (Camp, 1992; Conway, 1994). Similarly, Sommers's (1989) "writer's memo" compels students to describe their writing processes, identify their composing choices, and self-assess their writing. A variation of this strategy that highlights the importance of the social context of writing is Watson's (1991) letters on writing. The instructor and students write observations and questions about their writing processes, exchange letters, and respond in writing to each other's letters. This semester-long dialogue encourages a kind of "conversational scaffolding" that helps students to make decisions about their texts.

The postwrite may become most effective as a form of self-assessment if writers not only identify achievements and obstacles and set goals, but also subsequently follow up to see how well new goals were met. The postwrite, then, is not merely written, turned in with the essay, and never looked at again. It should be referred to periodically so the writer can judge for herself how much progress is being made. A self-assessment prompt that can be combined with the postwrite is a *checklist of strategies and goals* for the next draft or piece of writing. The checklist can guide further composing and be a starting place for the next postwrite. The checklist could also contain new strategies the writer would like to try out.

Shaping Self-Assessment Prompts. The point being emphasized through these strategies is that for self-assessment to guide effective revision, the act of assessment has to be a prelude to choice of a consequent strategy. A brief review of studies on revision strategies can help teachers shape the specific language of self-assessment prompts that will help writers detect problems and select appropriate strategies. Flower, Hayes, Carey, Shriver, and Stratman's (1986) analysis of expert writers' texts reveal two key variables underlying "expert performance": knowledge and intention. Expert writers have a command of different strategies that can be applied discriminately. In addition, expert writers are cognizant of the goals of the task and can adapt a task to their own goals and intentions. Thus, to revise effectively, novice writers need to be prompted to detect problems as they relate to task goals and to discover or invent strategies for writing their ways out of the problems.

Studies by Beach (1976, 1982), Park (1986), and Miller (1982) complement the findings of Flower and Hayes, particularly Beach and Eaton's (1984) work on factors influencing self-assessment. Students must be able to describe the social and rhetorical context of the writing assignment in order to assess their own writing—be able to describe their content goals, goals for the audience, and rhetorical strategies.

These research studies help us to devise a template for prompts that can guide students to consider different domains when they assess their own writing. The prompts can be used to guide development of the "postwrite" associated with portfolio content selection. However, they are just as applicable (and perhaps even more effective) when they guide self-assessment of a draft and function as a prelude to redrafting. Research suggests that any such template focus on two areas: cognitive growth and development of procedural skills.

Cognitive Growth.

- What new understandings about how writers write have you come to as you worked on this draft or piece?
- What did you do particularly well in this draft?
- How is this draft better than your earlier draft? [How is this piece an improvement over your earlier work?]
- What were the most important challenges in the draft/piece you think you handled well?

Beaven (1977) pointed out that asking students to identify new understanding about writing or writing strengths counteracts a culture in which students have been conditioned to see only their errors and failures. The ability to find something in their writing that has worked effectively is a self-motivating strategy: Students recognize achievement, seek improvement, and find something that has been personally satisfying. Finally, these prompts get students to develop both a global and a context- or discipline-specific understanding about writing.

Another critical area is helping students cross the bridge from one draft to the next, or one writing assignment to another:

- What are your plans for the next draft/piece of writing?
- What one thing will you do to improve your next draft/piece of writing?
- If you had more time to write this draft/piece, what would you do to continue working on it?

Individualized goal setting gives students more direct control over their writing: The responsibility for improvement is placed on the student, who follows through on decisions based on the previous self-assessment. Teachers need also to acknowledge that student authors often know best what areas require self-improvement. According to Beaven, asking students to focus on a few goals not only strengthens their capacity for risk taking, independent decision making, and goal setting, but also provides a focus for helping them achieve success. Thus, the practice of goal setting and returning to goals as criteria for improvement becomes a self-motivation strategy.

A final note about goal setting: The course syllabi in writing classes are often organized according to a well-intentioned sequence of rhetorical modes—for example, from personal narrative to persuasive arguments or research writing. We would like to suggest an alternative to traditional practice. If we understand the inherent values of self-assessment, we need to provide more opportunities for our students to pursue the goals and skills articulated in their postwrites in order for their self-assessments to take hold. Rather than trying new modes—for example, moving from a comparison/contrast essay to argumentative essay—students ought to be reworking their understandings of rhetorical context, audience, goals, and intentions through further work in a mode or genre they are exploring, usually by addressing additional topics. Students can then revisit their self-assessments from the previous assignment and evaluate the effectiveness of their strategies. Groups of students can address issues of strategy and context as they deal with similar assignments. Both strategies and evaluation criteria can be discussed by a full class, listed on charts, and reviewed at various points so that by the end of the sequence of assignments discussion can focus on global versus context-specific strategies and standards.

Procedural Skills Development.

- What problems did you encounter during the writing of this draft/piece?
- What solutions did you find for these problems?
- What new strategies did you try out with this draft/piece?
- What did you try to improve or experiment with in this draft/piece?

This category of prompts asks students to recognize, categorize, and diagnose problems in their texts, a step in the revision process that beginning writers often overlook. Flower et al. (1986) asserted that when students fail to analyze the weaknesses or problems in their texts, they "plunge" into surface-level substitutions such as paraphrasing instead of diagnosing and crafting a meaningful revision. For example, a student who detects that sentences in a paragraph "sound bad" may simply toy with word choices or sentence lengths. However, if the student diagnoses that certain sentences "do not fit logically with the rest of the paragraph," the student is in a better position to draw on a repertoire of relevant strategies (e.g., he can reread the entire piece and find a more appropriate place for the sentences, or he can recast the entire paragraph). Finally, the wordings of the prompts let students know what their teachers (and experienced writers) expect and value. For example, Beaven noted that by asking students to identify problems in the text, teachers also indicate that most, if not all, writers encounter difficulties. The latter question acknowledges that a capacity for risk taking is often a key to new learning and to improved writing.

Interrupting Typical Behavior. Developing appropriate prompts for self-assessment is only a first step. These prompts have to be integrated into the coursework and called up at the most opportune times. As mentioned earlier, one reason self-assessment works is because performing an assessment interrupts automatic behavior. If the interruption is an occasion for reflection and evaluation, self- or peer feedback, and goal setting activities, the writer can learn to effectively modify her behavior to produce the desired results.

Unfortunately, we can offer no broad prescription for identifying opportune times for interruption of stereotypic behavior. Teachers who know their students well and who encourage writing in class may be able to introduce an appropriate self-assessment prompt while students are actually composing. (The questions offered earlier can prompt "real-time" as well as postscript assessments.) In addition to written self-assessments, teachers can use conferences with students to prompt and guide self-assessment and can train writers to include out-loud self-assessments in peer groups.

To find the best "schedule" for interruption, teachers have to experiment. One possibility is very frequent interruption. Lewkowicz and Moon (1985), for example, described one study in which the writer self-assesses after drafting each sentence. The writer chooses from a list of 17 statements the statement that best describes the sentence she just wrote. For example: "The reader may not understand this," "This says exactly what I mean," "This doesn't give enough detail" (pp. 70–71). The writer also provides a short comment about why she believes that the statement is the best choice. Then, based on which statement was chosen, the student selects a remedial strategy from a list of nine possible strategies: "I think I'll leave it like this"; "I'd better cross this statement out and say it in a different way"; "I'd better find a way of linking this sentence with the other one." This method forces writers to systematically evaluate their writing and can help teachers discover at what point students are having problems. However, it is an extreme. It disrupts the flow of composing—perhaps to the point where the writer loses track of what she was trying to communicate in the first place. Teachers and students together have to decide what is the best schedule for self-assessment activities.

   Training and Practice. When first asked to self-assess their writing, students may not be able to define what they feel best about in their drafts or what their biggest obstacles were when writing. However, if students help define evaluation criteria when an assignment is made, they will probably begin to use the terminology and ideas from those discussions. We can "hear" such discussions behind these sample comments from students' postwrites in an introductory college-level writing course: "I tried my best to keep in mind the concept of cohesiveness. Every sentence that I wrote made me look at my previous sentence and see how they linked to one another"; "I think I made my sentences more cohesive so that one sentence was able to flow into the next." Clearly "cohesion" was the subject of a class discussion. As Lewkowicz and Moon (1985) noted, many students initially equate their goals with those of their teachers because they do not know how to set attainable goals of their own. Through training and practice, students will gradually internalize criteria that they can apply themselves, based on the requirements of the writing situation. In the case where the student and the teacher disagree, Lewkowicz and Moon suggested exploring the discrepancy because it should not automatically be assumed that the student's self-assessment is wrong.
   Because students may have difficulties setting appropriate goals by themselves, teachers have to devise training strategies, usually within the contexts of peer and student-teacher conferences. For example, a writer, after completing her draft, determined that she needed to reorganize her essay and that the section in an encyclopedia on her topic would be the best model for her new organization. After a quick discussion with her peer group about the nature of an argumentative essay, however, she decided to revise that item on her checklist to read, "In the next draft I will put my ideas in a different order with the most important example first, and the weak example in the middle."
   Finally, at the end of a course, instructors can ask students to write a carefully thought-out essay in which the students evaluate themselves as writers, or evaluate the contents of their writing portfolio, or both. In this "extended postwrite," students may respond to the same kinds of prompts, but reflect on an entire semester or year and think ahead to future writing tasks.

IS SELF-ASSESSMENT A PANACEA FOR WRITERS?

Is self-assessment a panacea? That may be a bit of an exaggeration. However, most studies in second language learning have determined that self-assessments are reliable and fairly accurate (Blanche & Merino, 1989; Rolfe, 1990). In fact, one study found that self-assessment questionnaires can place students into the appropriate class at least as well as commonly used standardized tests (LeBlanc & Painchaud, 1985).

Brindley (1989) reported that using self-assessment procedures can increase adult second language learners' motivation, help them become more goal-oriented, and help them learn to take responsibility for the assessment of their progress and ability. Self-assessment tasks also can increase the dialogue between the instructor and student (Lewis, 1990).

Two problems that second-language teachers have encountered using self-assessments are learners' lack of proper training and cultural or gender differences (e.g., aversion to "boasting"; fear of criticizing a male teacher's effectiveness) that hinder students' abilities to self-assess accurately and effectively (Blanche & Merino, 1989; Brindley, 1989; Lewis, 1990; Lewkowicz & Moon, 1985; Oskarsson, 1980; Rolfe, 1990). It seems that these barriers can be overcome. Culture-sensitive training and explanation of the process and rationale can help students who are hesitant to self-assess (LeBlanc & Painchaud, 1985). In addition, as we have suggested, students can learn how to use self-assessment approaches, should be given opportunities to practice the procedures, need help interpreting the results of their self-assessments, and need guidance in identifying subsequent courses of action and appropriate new goals.

Clearly, in the course of this chapter we have offered only hints as to what a research-guided practitioner might do to bring effective self-assessment into the writing classroom and into each writer's repertoire of strategies. We have said next to nothing about assignment design as it might relate to the personal value, or valence, students attach to particular pieces of writing. We have said little about enhancing students' motivation to improve, or about the breaking of complex rhetorical situations into parts. Nonetheless, we hope that the questions and examples we have provided will guide teachers (and researchers) who want to explore the potentials for self-assessment in writing instruction.

What will motivate teachers to engage in such an exploration? Reflective self-assessment, of course!

REFERENCES

Atwell, N. (1987). *In the middle: Writing, reading, and learning with adolescents*. Portsmouth, NH: Heineman.

Badger, L., Dilena, M., Peters, J., Webster, C., & Weeks, B. (1991). *Literacy assessment in practice: Language arts*. Education Department of Adelaide, South Australia.

Beach, R. (1976). Self-evaluation strategies of extensive revisers and non-revisers. *Composition Communication, 27*, 160–164.

Beach, R. (1982). The pragmatics of self-assessing. In R. A. Sudol (Ed.), *Revising: New essays for teachers of writing* (71-83). Urbana, IL: National Council of Teachers of English.

Beach, R., & Anson, C. (1988). The pragmatics of memo writing: Developmental differences in the use of rhetorical strategies. *Written Communication, 5*, 157-183.

Beach, R., & Eaton, S. (1984). Factors influencing self-assessing and revising by college freshmen. In R. Beach & L.S. Bridwell (Eds.), *New directions in composition research*. New York: Guilford.

Beaven, M. H. (1977). Individualized goal setting, self-evaluation, and peer evaluation. In C. R. Cooper & L. Odell (Eds.), *Evaluating writing: Describing, measuring, judging* (pp. 135-156). Urbana, IL: National Council of Teachers of English.

Bellack, A.S., Rozensky, R., & Schwartz, J. (1974). A comparison of two forms of self-monitoring in a behavioral weight reduction program. *Behavior Therapy, 5*, 523-550.

Berlin, J. (1987). *Rhetoric and reality: Writing instruction in American colleges, 1900-1985*. Carbondale: Southern Illinois University Press.

Bissex, G. (1980). *GNYS AT WRK: A child learns to write and read*. Cambridge, MA: Harvard University Press.

Blanche, P., & Merino, B. J. (1989). Self-assessment of foreign-language skills: Implications for teachers and researchers. *Language Learning: A Journal of Applied Linguistics, 39*, 313-340.

Bornstein, P., Hamilton, S., & Bornstein M. T. (1986). Self-monitoring procedures. In A. Ciminero, K. Calhoun, & H. Adams (Eds.), *Handbook of behavioral assessment* (3rd ed., pp. 176-222). New York: Wiley.

Bridwell, L. (1980). Revising strategies in twelfth grade students' transactional writing. *Research in the Teaching of English, 14*, 197-222.

Brindley, G. (1989). *Assessing achievement in the learner-centered curriculum*. Sydney: National Centre for English Language Teaching and Research.

Bruffee, K. (1984). Collaborative learning and the "conversation of mankind." *College English, 47*, 635-652.

Bruffee, K. (1986). *A short course in writing* (3rd ed.). Boston: Little, Brown and Company.

Calkins, L.M. (1986). *The art of teaching writing.* Portsmouth, NH: Heineman.

Camp, R. (1992). Portfolio reflections. In K. Yancey (Ed.), *Portfolios in the writing classroom: An introduction* (pp. 61-79). Urbana, IL: National Council of Teachers of English.

Cavior, N., & Marabott, C.M. (1976). Monitoring verbal behaviors in a dyadic interaction. *Journal of Consulting and Clinical Psychology, 44,* 68-76.

Cochran-Smith, M., & Lytle, S. (1993). *Inside/outside: Teacher research and knowledge.* New York: Teachers College Press.

Connell, M.C., & Carta, J.J. (1993). Programming generalization of in-class transition skills: Teaching preschoolers with developmental delays to self-assess and recruit contingent teacher praise. *Journal of Applied Behavior Analysis, 26,* 345-352.

Conway, G. (1994). Portfolio cover letters, students' self-presentation, and teachers' ethics. In L. Black, D. Daiker, J. Sommers, & G. Stygall (Eds.), *New directions in portfolio assessment: Reflective practice, critical theory, and large-scale scoring* (pp. 83-92). Portsmouth, NH: Heineman.

Daiker, D., & Morenberg, M. (Eds.). (1990). *The writing teacher as researcher: Essays in the theory & practice of class-based research.* Portsmouth, NH: Boynton/Cook Publishers.

Dyson, A. (1983). The role of oral language in early writing processes. *Research in the Teaching of English, 17,* 1-30.

Elbow, P. (1981). *Writing with power: Techniques for mastering the writing process.* New York: Oxford University Press.

Emig, J. (1971). *The composing processes of twelfth graders.* Urbana, IL: National Council of Teachers of English.

Flower, L. (1979). Writer-based prose: A cognitive basis for problems in writing. *College English, 41,* 19-37.

Flower, L., & Hayes, J.R. (1981a). A cognitive process theory of writing. *College Composition & Communication, 32,* 365-387.

Flower, L., & Hayes, J.R. (1981b). The pregnant pause: An inquiry into the nature of planning. *Research in the Teaching of English, 15,* 229-243.

Flower, L., Hayes, J.R., Carey, L., Shriver, K., & Stratman, J. (1986). Detection, diagnosis, and the strategies of revision. *College Composition and Communication, 37,* 16-55.

Fredericksen, L.W., Epstein, L.H., & Kosevsky, B.P. (1975). Reliability and controlling effects of three procedures for self-monitoring smoking. *Psychological Record, 25,* 255-264.

Goswami, D., & Stillman, P. R. (Eds.). (1987). *Reclaiming the classroom: Teacher research as an agency for change.* Upper Montclair, NJ: Boynton/Cook.

Graves, D. (1983). *Teachers & children at work.* Portsmouth, NH: Heinemann.

Hansen, J., Newkirk, T., & Graves, D. (Eds.). (1985). *Breaking ground: Teachers relate reading and writing in the elementary school.* Portsmouth, NH: Heineman.

Hawai'i Department of Education. (1994). *Hawai'i writing assessment scoring rubric* (draft). Honolulu, HI.

Herman, J.L., Aschbacher, P.R., & Winters, L. (1992). *A practical guide to alternative assessment.* Alexandria, VA: Association for Supervision and Curriculum Development.

Hilgers, T. (1984). Toward a taxonomy of beginning writers' evaluative statements on written compositions. *Written Communication, 1,* 365-384.

Hilgers, T. (1986). How children change as critical evaluators of writing: Four three-year case studies. *Research in the Teaching of English, 20,* 36-55.

Hoon, P. W. (1976). Effects of self-monitoring and self-recording on ecological acts. *Psychological Reports, 38,* 1285-1286.

Hussey, E., Bayer, A., Hilgers, T., & Jones, K. (1995). *Writing in Hawai'i high school senior classes: A glimpse into a few windows* (Report No. 2). Honolulu, HI: Office of Faculty Development and Academic Support.

Johnson, S.M., & White, G. (1971). Self-observation as an agent of behavioral change. *Behavior Therapy, 2,* 488-497.

Kanfer, F.H. (1975). Self-management methods. In F. H. Kanfer & A. P. Goldstein (Eds.), *Helping people change: A textbook of methods* (pp. 309-355). New York: Pergamon.

Kanfer, F.H., & Phillips, J.S. (1966). Behavior therapy: A panacea for all ills or a passing fancy? *Archives of General Psychiatry, 15,* 114-128.

Kazdin, A. E. (1974). Self-monitoring and behavior change. In M. J. Mahoney & C. E. Thorensen (Eds.), *Self-control: Power to the person* (pp. 218-246). Monterey, CA: Brooks-Cole.

Knoblauch, C.H., & Brannon, L. (1984). *Rhetorical traditions and the teaching of writing.* Upper Montclair, NJ: Boynton/Cook Publishers.

Kopp, J. (1988). Self-monitoring: A literature review of research and practice. *Social Work Research Abstracts, 24*(4), 8-20.

Larson, R. L. (1971). The evaluation of teaching college English. *ERIC Clearinghouse on the Teaching of English in Higher Education.* New York: Modern Language Association of America.

LeBlanc, R., & Painchaud, G. (1985). Self-assessment as a second language placement instrument. *TESOL Quarterly, 19,* 673-687.

LeMahieu, P., & Foss, H. (1994). Standards at the base of school reform. *School Administrator, 51*(5), 16–22.

Lewis, J. (1990). Self-assessment in the classroom: A case study. In G. Brindley (Ed.), *The second language curriculum in action* (pp. 187-213). Sydney: National Centre for English Language Teaching and Research.

Lewkowicz, J. A., & Moon, J. (1985). Evaluation: A way of involving the learner. In J. C. Alderson (Ed.), *Evaluation* (pp. 45-80). Oxford: Pergamon.

Lipinski, D.P., Black, J.L., Nelson, R.O., & Ciminero, A.R. (1975). Influence of motivational variables on the reactivity and reliability of self-recording. *Journal of Consulting and Clinical Psychology, 43*, 637-646.

Mahoney, M.J., Moore, B.S., Wade, T.C., & Moura, N.G. (1973). The effects of continuous and intermittent self-monitoring on academic behavior. *Journal of Consulting and Clinical Psychology, 41*, 65-69.

McFall, R.M. (1970). The effects of self-monitoring on normal smoking behavior. *Journal of Consulting and Clinical Psychology, 35*, 135-142.

McFall, R.M., & Hammen, C.L. (1971). Motivation, structure, and self-monitoring: The role of nonspecific factors in smoking reduction. *Journal of Consulting and Clinical Psychology, 37*, 80-86.

Miller, S. (1982). How writers evaluate their own writing. *College Composition and Communication, 33*, 176-183.

Nelson, R. O., Lipinski, D. P., & Black, J. L. (1976). The relative reactivity of external observations and self-monitoring. *Behavior Therapy, 7*, 314-321.

Newkirk, T. (1982). Young writers as critical readers. *Language Arts, 59*, 451-457.

Nold, E. (1980). Revising: Intentions and conventions. In R. Sudol (Ed.), *Revising*. Urbana, IL: National Council of Teachers of English.

Oskarsson, M. (1980). *Approaches to self-assessment in foreign language learning*. Oxford: Pergamon.

Park, D. (1986). Analyzing audiences. *College Composition & Communication, 37*, 478–488.

Richards, C. S., McReynolds, W. T., Holt, S., & Sexton, T. (1976a). Effects on information feedback and self-administered consequences on self-monitoring study behavior. *Journal of Counseling Psychology, 23*, 316-321.

Richards, C. S., Perri, M. G., & Gortney, C. (1976b). Increasing the maintenance of self-control treatments through faded counselor contact and high information feedback. *Journal of Counseling Psychology, 23*, 405-406.

Rief, L. (1991). *Seeking diversity: Language arts with adolescents.* Portsmouth, NH: Heineman.

Rolfe, T. (1990). Self- and peer-assessment in the ESL curriculum. In G. Brindley (Ed.), *The second language curriculum in action* (pp. 163-186). Sydney: National Centre for English Language Teaching and Research.

Routman, R. (1991). *Invitations: Changing as teachers and learners K-12.* Portsmouth, NH: Heinemann Educational Books.

Schön, D. A. (1987). *Educating the reflective practitioner.* San Francisco: Jossey-Bass.

Sommers, J. (1989). The writer's memo: Collaboration, response, and development. In C. Anson (Ed.), *Writing and response: Theory, practice, and research* (pp. 174-186). Urbana, IL: National Council of Teachers of English.

Sommers, N. (1980). Revision strategies of student writers and experienced adult writers. *College Composition & Communication, 31,* 378-388.

Tharp, R.G., & Wetzel, R.J. (1969). *Behavior modification in the natural environment.* New York: Academic Press.

Watson, S. (1991). Letters on writing—A medium of exchange with students of writing. In K. Adams & J. Adams (Eds.), *Teaching advanced composition: Why and how* (pp. 133-150). Portsmouth, NH: Boynton/Cook Publishers.

Weaver, C. (1990). *Understanding whole language: From principles to practice.* Portsmouth, NH: Heinemann Educational Books.

White, E. M. (1994). *Teaching and assessing writing: Recent advances in understanding, evaluating, and improving student performance* (2nd ed.). San Francisco: Jossey-Bass.

White, E. M. (1995). *Assigning, responding, evaluating: A writing teacher's guide* (3rd ed.). New York: St. Martin's Press.

Zimmerman, J., & Levitt, E.E. (1975). Why not give your client a counter: A survey of what happened when we did. *Behaviour Research and Therapy, 13,* 333-337.

2

STUDENT SELF-ASSESSMENT: SOME ISSUES AND CONCERNS FROM POSTMODERN AND FEMINIST PERSPECTIVES*

Susan Latta
University of Detroit-Mercy

Janice Lauer
Purdue University

As educators, we are naturally concerned with fostering the growth of our students in as many ways as possible. In accordance with our concern for encouraging critical thinking and reflection, many of us are experimenting with various ways of using self-reflective writing by students to help them assess the nature of their interactions with the learning environments we provide. Such works of student self-assessment can be used in many ways: to assess a student's increasing understanding of an area of study; to chart a student's cognitive and affective development over the course of her education; and to examine growth in ability, such as in writing portfolios. In addition, as Eaton and Pougiales (1993) noted, the opportunity for students to engage in such self-analysis provides definite benefits for them as well. Students can begin to be in more control of their learning experience, making learning an intrinsic motivation rather than an extrinsic one. Students also can share responsibility for evaluation with the teacher by voicing their feelings concerning their work and its quality. As we look for more ways to engage students in our courses, to invite them to take active roles in their education, student self-assessment activities in our curricula provide an excellent opportunity to encourage these goals.

However, just as we want our students to be more critical and self-aware concerning their experiences in the classroom, we must be

*Many of the conflicts discussed in this chapter are represented in Emig and Phelps (1995).

willing to engage in such critical and self-reflective practices ourselves as we choose our pedagogical practices and structure our curricula. With the growing influence of various postmodern and feminist theories on educational practice, we need to consider the possibility that these theories may provide us with insights and new perspectives on our current practices that could enable us to make the process of student self-assessment even more profitable that it currently is. This essay, therefore, examines what we can learn from postmodern and feminist approaches, especially in terms of the challenges students face when writing such self-reflective pieces.

SELF-ASSESSMENT: WHAT EXACTLY DO WE MEAN?

Here are three questions we must consider when we ask students to engage in self-assessment activities:

1. Which "self" or "selves," or subject positions, are we asking students to assess? Do we know? Do they?
2. What happens if the "self," or the subject position, the student assesses is not the "self" the teacher or institution is attempting to inscribe?
3. What do we mean when we ask students to engage in the act of self-assessment?

THE SELF AS A SOCIAL CONSTRUCTION: THE TENSION BETWEEN THE INDIVIDUAL AND THE COMMUNITY

One of the key conflicts that has defined the clash between competing theories of composition, and which reflects a growing concern in other fields as well, is the tension between the individual and the community. A key example of this in composition studies is the firestorm of responses provoked by Hairston's attack on postmodern, feminist, and political approaches to writing—approaches that, she felt, imposed a content and ideology on student writers that negated their sense of agency and autonomy as learners. It is also this same sense of the autonomous agency of the learner and the writer that drives most of our goals in asking students to engage in self-assessment activities: to increase a self-awareness of their abilities, growth, and accomplishments; to take control of their learning experiences. Seemingly, then, the goals of postmodern and feminist theories would be in conflict with the goals of self-reflection because they call into question the very nature of the autonomous self. However, postmodern and feminist approaches to the issues of self and subjectivity do not necessarily negate an individual's agency; rather, some theorists argue that postmodern and feminist approaches further encourage the possibility for action, growth, and change.

Over the past decade, more and more of our practices as teachers, and especially as teachers of writing, have been influenced by our field's growing interest in various postmodern and feminist theories of language, reality, and subjectivity (see Berlin, 1988; Faigley, 1986; Miller, 1989). This influence is particularly apparent in theories of the social construction of knowledge through language (see Bruffee, 1986; LeFevre, 1987; Leff, 1978). The transmission model of language, the belief that language is a medium through which truths can be communicated, has been called into question by theories that hold that language shapes both us and the cultures we have developed (Faigley, 1986). As a result, social views of writing argue that composing is a contextual act inextricably linked through language with particular social, cultural, and historical moments in which writers write.

Bizzell (1982) has explained that such social theories of writing lead to an understanding of the writer as a socially constituted subjectivity, the product of her interactions in the many communities in which she finds herself. Although this unique combination of influences produces a particular cluster of subject positions, these subjectivities are bound by the limits of the communities to which she belongs:

> The individual is already inside a discourse community when she learns a native tongue, since the infant does not learn some generalized form of language but rather the habits of language use in the neighborhood, or the discourse community into which she is born. Since this discourse community already possesses traditional, shared ways of understanding experience, the infant doesn't learn to conceptualize in a social vacuum, either, but is constantly being advised by more mature community members whether her inferences are correct, whether her groupings of experiential data into evidence are significant, and so on. (p. 217)

Writers cannot step outside of their social, cultural, and historical communities when they write; neither can they when engaged in self-assessment.

Although these external influences would seem to strip the subject of any sense of agency, leaving her at the mercy of deterministic forces, many postmodern and feminist theorists argue that this is not the case. Butler (1990), for example, has argued that the view of the socially constituted subject suggests agency and change, for it eliminates the trap of essentialism. First, she argued that if we assume there is a subject outside a cultural field, we must assume that the only notion of agency possible is "prediscursive," that is, the subject actually exists before it is inscribed by the culture. Second, regarding the view that if one is constituted by the discourse, one is determined solely by the discourse, Butler noted:

> The enabling conditions for an assertion of "I" are provided by the structure of signification, the rules that regulate the legitimate and illegitimate invocation of that pronoun, the practices that establish the terms of intelligibility by which that pronoun can circulate. (p. 143)

The notions of legitimate and illegitimate, therefore, can be modified by a change in the signification system, a change that can be initiated by the individuals within that system. Thus, identity becomes a "practice," the self constructed by "a taking up of the tools [of language] where they lie, where the very 'taking up' is enabled by the tool lying there" (Butler, 1990, p. 145).

The conflict between competing subject positions can tremendously impact writers, both positively and negatively. Lauer (1994), for example, discussed some of the problems students and teachers have when writing to public discourse communities. By acknowledging these conflicts and contradictions, writers can become aware of the influences that shape them and begin to work on ways to come to terms with these influences.

A specific example of this is the difficulties many women experience in both their professional and personal lives. One of the key tenets of feminist research is that the roles which women in our society have been socialized to assume may place some of them at a disadvantage when attempting to enter academic and professional communities that have so long been dominated by men, and that this socialization can have an important impact on a woman's writing (see Crawford & Chaffin, 1986; Frey, 1990; Gilbert & Gubar, 1992; Gubar, 1981). Many women have found, after having been raised to see their roles in society in general as emphasizing cooperation, negotiation, and nurturing, that their difficulty in adapting to the often agonistic and competitive modes of discourse which predominate in academic communities can lead to conflicts. Cayton (1990), for example, has shown in her study of undergraduate writers that gender roles and corresponding cognitive differences in ways of knowing the world (see Belenky, Clinchy, Goldberger, & Tarule, 1986) can lead to writer's block in women writers. Flynn (1990) and Kirsch (1993) have also shown that even when women writers are able to adapt to the conventions of their particular academic communities, they still feel uneasiness and self-doubt about their abilities and, because they often attempt to work out these conflicts in their academic work, find themselves in the uncomfortable position of risking their status and authority by questioning the communities to which they belong and by attempting to negotiate texts within these communities that allow for alternative voices and forms. Current research by Latta (1995) suggests that some novice women writers in professional academic discourse communities often find themselves experiencing blocks or high levels of writing anxiety when faced with a situation where they perceive that the views and beliefs of their evaluators conflict with their own and that their evaluators do not value either their positions or the forms that their arguments take.

If we add to our consideration of possible subject positions that the writer may assume other social and cultural factors than gender, such as race, religion, socioeconomic class, family background and beliefs, and so forth, we can see how finding appropriate voices in writing becomes a difficult task. This also complicates the issue of self-assessment, for when we ask a student to assess her "self," exactly which self is she supposed to assess?

ASSESSING OUR "SELVES": WHAT DO WE MEAN?

Another common tenet in recent postmodern and feminist theory is the calling into question the very notion of a text. A text can be an essay, a movie, a culture, a class, ourselves. What texts are, and how they might be assessed, is therefore called into question because the belief that a reader can discern one "correct" reading of a text becomes problematic. As reader-response theory has shown, because we each have different clusters of subject positions, we bring to a text differing backgrounds, beliefs, and experiences. Because of these differing backgrounds, our interpretations will differ—a fact that we as instructors have long known. In addition, if the communities to which our students belong do not share the values and beliefs of academic institutions, we are faced with a possible double bind: Whose conventions will prevail? Usually it is the conventions of the academic community that prevail—standards which as feminists have pointed out, inscribe the dominant language and epistemologies of the patriarchy and, as many Marxists have noted, inscribe elitist and classist assumptions.

Faigley (1992) has related the case of a student writing an entrance exam in the early years of this century who, despite meeting the minimum requirements of essay assignment, received a failing grade because one of the stories he chose to analyze revealed, according to the Commission on English's report, "that his chief interest . . . is in stories that are trivial and sensational" (p. 117). Faigley pointed out that what was at issue in this case was not the criteria often cited in the assessment of student texts, such as thesis, development, and organization, for the failed essay exhibited adequate control of these. Rather, the essay failed to acknowledge the discourse community's accepted view on popular literature as "trivial and sensational." Therefore, the student failed the essay because he failed to understand that as a prospective member of the academic community, he was expected to assume a particular subject position, a position that was an unstated, but very important, criterion for assessment.

Student self-assessment, therefore, could provide students with the opportunity to clarify for themselves the differences between their understandings of academic expectations and their own, an opportunity for students to genuinely engage with the academic institution on their own terms and to offer them a possible forum for critique. In several accounts of types of self-assessment prompts and assignments, we see that instructors are beginning to acknowledge this and to ask students to consider the role of the institution and its expectations on their learning experience. For example, students in the capstone seminar at Fairhaven College at Washington University complete a self-evaluation that invites them to "pay attention both to ways in which the institution helped or hindered their progress and to their own developing knowledge of their subject matter and themselves as learners" (Waluconis 1993, p. 29).

STUDENT SELF-ASSESSMENT: SOME TENTATIVE SUGGESTIONS

First, the social constructionist view that writers and learners can assume many different subject positions calls on us to make clear which "self" or "selves" are being evaluated. If we emphasize that the writing of our students, including their self-assessments, is rhetorically situated, and provide them with writing opportunities that occur within a rhetorically plausible situation, students can discuss the different roles that diverse writing and learning situations entail and can examine the ways in which readers occasion the voices that they will assume. We can also ask students to think critically about the roles that they assume in these situations and the ethical, moral, and political implications of them. Students can also examine the conventions of the discourse communities in which they write and the forums in which their works appear, thereby enabling them to be more explicit about the criteria by which the institution judges their work and the judgments they make. In composition studies, Porter (1994) has developed the *forum analysis*, a method based on Foucault's theories of discourse and power, that not only enables students to learn the conventions of the academic community in which they are writing, but also provides them with the opportunity to critique those communities by considering what can and cannot be said in these communities, who is allowed to speak and who is silenced. Such a method encourages students to think critically about the ways that academic culture has shaped them as learners and writers.

Second we must acknowledge that often we do not give students adequate instruction in how to assess their own texts and their growth as writers. Just as we no longer assume that students will somehow magically learn to write by only reading and discussing essays, and therefore provide planning, peer response, and revision to guide them through the process, correspondingly we cannot assume that students will somehow learn how to evaluate their own work without guidance. Just as teachers have come to realize the difficulty students have in responding to other students' texts during peer review and that they need guidance in making appropriate and helpful responses to student texts through modeling successful peer-group strategies, similarly our students need guidance in how to choose their "best" work or to write self-reflective essays examining their growth as writers.

Third, students need help in realizing that sometimes the roles they want to assume in their writing may conflict with the roles that they are required by institutional guidelines to assume. Students, for example, need to see that writing in personal discourse communities about traumatic personal events such as rape, a friend's suicide, parental abuse, and drug addiction entails conventional expectations different from those of academic discourse communities. For those of us who use portfolios, we emphasize student ownership and the student's right to make choices as to how their work will progress and be presented, but students also need to know the expectations of portfolio assessors. By understanding what these broad guidelines are, students can better anticipate what the consequences will be if they do not meet institutional requirements. Making self-assessment and reflection an integral part of our classes and discussing openly and critically with students the intent and uses of such self-assessments will help them better understand their choices and the consequences of those choices.

Finally, we must also ask ourselves about the implications of assigning student self-assessments. Many students find assessment and evaluation of themselves in any setting to be hostile. For example, research in writing apprehension has shown that apprehension increases when students are faced with the possibility of evaluation (Daly &

Wilson, 1983). Will asking students to assess themselves alleviate this pressure, or will it exacerbate their already present anxieties about themselves as learners and writers? In addition, by asking students to assess themselves, are we asking them to internalize the strictures and guidelines of a system that may be discriminatory; what are the implications of this possibility both for them and for us?

To engage in critical self-reflection, as we ask our students to do in their self-assessments, is an important and worthy goal, and one that we should continue to encourage in our students. At the same time, we should also be self-critical of our own practices, including our own self-assessment.

REFERENCES

Belenky, M. F., Clinchy B. M., Goldberger, N. R., & Tarule, J. M. (1986). *Women's ways of knowing; the development of self, voice, and mind.* New York: Basic Books.

Berlin, J. (1988). Rhetoric and ideology in the writing class. *College English, 50*(5), 477–494.

Bizzell, P. (1982). Cognition, convention, and certainty: What we need to know about writing. *Pre/Text, 3*(3), 213–243.

Bruffee, K. (1986). Social construction, language, and the authority of knowledge: A bibliographic essay. *College English, 48*(8), 773–790.

Butler, J. (1990). *Gender trouble: Feminism and the subversion of identity.* New York: Routledge.

Cayton, M. K. (1990). What happens when things go wrong: Women and writing blocks. *Journal of Advanced Composition, 10*(2), 321–337.

Crawford, M., & Chaffin, R. (1986). The reader's construction of meaning: Cognitive research on gender and comprehension. In P. Schweickart & E. Flynn (Eds.), *Gender and reading: Essays on readers, texts, and contexts* (pp. 3–30). Baltimore: Johns Hopkins University Press.

Daly, J., & Wilson, D. (1983). Writing apprehension, self-esteem, and personality. *Research in the Teaching of English, 17,* 427–441.

Eaton, M., & Pougiales, R. (1993). Work, reflection, and community: Conditions that support writing self-evaluations. *New Directions for Teaching and Learning, 56,* 47–63.

Emig, J., & Phelps, L. (Eds.). (1995). *Feminine principles and women's experience: American composition and rhetoric.* Pittsburgh: University of Pittsburgh Press.

Faigley, L. (1986). Competing theories of process: A critique and proposal. *College English, 48*(6), 527–542.

Faigley, L. (1992). *Fragments of rationality: Postmodernity and the subject of composition.* Pittsburgh: University of Pittsburgh Press.

Flynn, E. (1990). Composing "Composing as a woman": A perspective on research. *College Composition and Communication, 41,* 83–89.

Frey, O. (1990). Beyond literary Darwinism: Women's voices and critical discourse. *College English, 52,* 507–526.

Gllbert, S., & Gubar, S. (1992). Infection in the sentence: The woman writer and the anxiety of authorship. In R. Warhol & D.P. Herndl (Eds.), *Feminisms: An anthology of literary theory and criticism* (pp. 289–300). New Brunswick, NJ: Rutgers University Press.

Gubar, S. (1981). The "blank page" and the issue of female creativity. *Critical Inquiry, 3,* 243–263.

Kirsch, G. (1993). *Women writing the academy: Audience, authority, and transformation.* Carbondale: Southern Illinois University Press.

Latta, S. (1995). *Women and writer's block: An exploration of social and cultural influences upon the writing processes of five graduate student writers.* Unpublished doctoral dissertation, Purdue University.

Lauer, J. (1994). Persuasive writing on public issues. In R. Winterowd & U. Gillespie (Eds.), *Composition in context: Essays in honor of Donald Stewart* (pp. 62-72). Carbondale: Southern Illinois University Press.

LeFevre, K. (1987). *Invention as a social act.* Carbondale: Southern Illinois University Press.

Leff, M. (1978). In search of Ariadne's Thread: A review of the recent literature on rhetorical theory. *Central States Speech Journal, 28,* 73-91.

Miller, S. (1989). *Rescuing the subject: A critical introduction to rhetoric and the writer.* Carbondale: Southern Illinois University Press.

Porter, J. (1994). *Audience and rhetoric.* Englewood Cliffs, NJ: Prentice-Hall.

Waluconis, C.J. (1993). Self-evaluation: Settings and uses. *New Directions for Teaching and Learning, 56,* 15-34.

3 APPLICATIONS AND ASSUMPTIONS OF STUDENT SELF-ASSESSMENT*

Rebecca Moore Howard

Texas Christian University

Composition curricula have traditionally been structured on judgments made about, not by, students. Some pedagogies do prompt students to make judgments about themselves—a practice commonly characterized as "self-assessment"—but these judgments are usually intended to affect only the writer, the self-assessor. Despite these established traditions, however, student self-assessment can be designed to produce more than writer-internal, immanent outcomes. Used as a means of composition course placement, student self-assessment asserts that writers' judgments about themselves can have writer-external meaning.

Because student self-assessment as a means of composition course placement is an unusual curricular protocol, in this chapter I survey scholarship on self-assessment in an effort to discover how self-assessment for course placement accords with and diverges from established theories and practices. As a necessary corollary to advocating this particular curricular innovation, I explore two discursive domains: definitions of *self* that underlie self-assessment in particular and the teaching of composition in general; and the signifying practice of "ability grouping," the familiar and seemingly "natural" way to place students in a hierarchized composition curriculum. My description of a

*My heartfelt thanks to Lynn Waldman, the administrator who was willing to implement a pilot program of composition course placement based on student self-assessment; to Margaret Flanders Darby, who energetically responded to my early ruminations on the problems of ability grouping; and to Kathleen Blake Yancey, who helped me realize some of the more important implications of my argument in this chapter.

curriculum that currently uses a combination of standardized test scores and student self-assessment for composition course placement describes the social and rhetorical stakes of such a model, reflects on the curricular quandaries that the model remedies, and also proposes ways in which it might be improved.

AN OVERVIEW OF SELF-ASSESSMENT

Self-assessment has long been regarded as an important component of revising: Writers who can assess their own prose can successfully revise that prose. Beach (1976) has been particularly active in pursuing this possibility, asserting that a goal of composition pedagogy should be to teach students "to critically evaluate their own writing" (p. 160) and that teachers' responses to drafts are an insufficient prompt for effective student revising (Beach, 1989). His various publications on the subject persuasively argue the value of self-assessment in revising and therefore in improving one's writing. His work is part of the literature on self-assessment that would involve students not in the assessment of self but in the assessment of their texts. Beaven (1977) also describes self-assessment in terms of text assessment.

Some composition scholars, however, do address the assessment of one's self. McCarthy, Meier, and Rinderer (1985) would have students assess their "abilities" (which, as I argue later in this chapter, are part of the "self") as an "important facet of the writing process" in order to precipitate beliefs and behaviors that will enable them to "write well." As a means of facilitating self-assessment, McCarthy et al. would have students fill out questionnaires that ask questions like "Can you write sentences in which the subjects and verbs are in agreement?" (p. 471). Implicit in such questions is a definition of "writing well" that privileges decontextualized mechanical correctness.

In contrast to the context-free self-assessment questions asked by McCarthy et al., the pedagogies of journal writing and portfolio evaluation establish contexts for student self-assessment. Typically these pedagogies involve students in self-assessment aimed at fostering a meta-understanding of themselves as writers in order to foster greater control over their writing processes. Like the analytic of McCarthy et al., the pedagogies of journal writing and portfolio evaluation do involve assessment of one's self—but it is self-assessment chiefly for immanent, writer-internal purposes. Self-assessment in journal writing and portfolio evaluation (which are described in some detail later in this chapter) may take context into account, but the outcome of the assessment is usually intended to affect only the writer, not the context.

In addition to the self-assessment outcomes of better revising or a meta-understanding of oneself as writer, I propose a third possible objective toward which student self-assessment might be deployed: composition course placement. Not only can self-assessment prompt a greater understanding of one's texts and one's self, but as a component of composition course placement it may explicitly prompt writers to consider themselves in dialogic relation to their peers and readers. Moreover, involving students in their own composition course placement asserts a writer-external meaning for self-assessment: It is not only useful to the individual writer, but it is "true" in a way that is meaningful beyond what we take to be the boundaries of the individual. Self-assessment is sufficiently "true" that composition curricula can be structured on it. Thus self-assessment in composition course placement would involve the writer not just in accounting for context (a time-honored objective of composition pedagogy) but also in affecting it.

THE "SELF" WHO WILL ASSESS

Two sets of contemporary theories raise problems for those who would engage students in self-assessment. One of these, the assertion that subjects do not exert agency but are instead constructed in and by language, would contradict the possibility that writers can exert the agency requisite to assessing themselves. The other, the assertion that higher education acts to reproduce and preserve the power of the dominant group, would suggest that any student self-assessment would merely affirm and reproduce the student's hierarchical place in the educational establishment. Both of these sets of theories exert considerable contemporary influence and must enter into a discussion of self-assessment. As a result of that dialogue, self-assessment theories and practices might become an important site for exploring slippage between what are commonly characterized as the binary oppositions of *self* and *other* and for finding the places where the hegemony of the institution can be pulled apart, its normative impulses countered by practices that represent students as subjects rather than objects.

The assertion that subjects do not exert agency but are instead constructed in and by language is commonly associated with and attributed to postmodern theory.[1] Commentators such as Worsham (1991)

---

[1] *Postmodernism*, Freisinger notes, is a "problematic, definitionally complex, and ideologically loaded" term (p. 242). I hesitate to use it here but plunge ahead anyway, propelled by the need for some sort of label that can serve as a signpost for the ideas I am discussing. For those who wish to pursue the complexities, Freisinger offers a useful overview.

have observed that postmodern theory contradicts the dominant semantic order of composition studies, in which writers are presumed susceptible of instruction that will give them control over their prose, themselves, and their world. Reviewing Clara Juncker's and Robert de Beaugrande's attempts to apply postmodern French feminism (*écriture féminine*) to composition studies, Worsham identifies contradictory philosophical orientations. Whereas French feminism shares the postmodern incredulity toward the possibility of communication, consensus, and control, instead promoting laughter, parody, and the subversion of order, composition studies acts on the modernist ideals of agency in the subject (one who originates and controls his or her own actions) and system in the world. Even when composition studies endeavors to embrace *écriture féminine*, it transforms postmodernity into political discourse, appropriating (and thus deforming) *écriture féminine* for the received purposes of composition studies rather than employing it as a means of examining, interrogating, and perhaps revising those purposes.

In contrast to Worsham, Flannery (1991) does find postmodern perspectives in composition studies: She encounters postmodernism in composition *theory* and modernism in composition *pedagogy*. Despite the impress of postmodernism on contemporary composition theory, she says, composition pedagogy works from cognitive and social constructionist models.

Postmodern composition theory challenges the notion of writers as originary agents, of writers as the source of their own writing. Instead, both writers and writing are products of the discourse environment.[2] Postmodern composition theory also challenges the notion of writers as unified subjects whose identity is coherent and consistent across contexts (which raises profound difficulty for those who would conduct context-free assessment of writing "abilities"). Most importantly for student self-assessment, postmodern composition theory challenges the notion of writers as agents, as potential "masters" of their own actions. Yet the social constructionist pedagogy gaining currency among compositionists does attribute agency (and hence individuality) if not originality to the subject: writers can be taught to understand and control their writing. Yancey and Spooner (1994) in their conclusion to a volume that reflects on the problem of the self in composition, articulates just how vexed yet necessary this notion is to the teaching of writing.

---

[2]The assertion that writers and writing are products of the discourse environment has the potential of making a quantity of significant trouble for the traditional assumptions of composition pedagogy. It raises, for example, interesting questions about—and inevitably challenges the very possibility of— plagiarism.

Bazerman (1992) articulates a precept that both postmodernism and social constructionism share (for in fact the two can never be neatly teased apart) when he advocates reflexivity, "a self-conscious praxis of language" (p. 36). He does not want that reflexivity to end in a "hall of mirrors," though—in the indeterminacy with which postmodernism is so often charged. Instead, he wants people to be able "to figure out where they stand and what they can say" (p. 37). He wants to retain the possibility of agency. That social constructionists represent the selves who participate in writing instruction as being constructed through social action does not necessarily deter them from simultaneously representing those selves as autonomous agents capable of choosing and changing their own identities—their own selves—by changing the social organism that constructs them.

From Worsham's (1991) perspective, the postmodern interrogation of agency (at least that of French feminism) opposes the traditional aims of composition studies. From Flannery's (1991) perspective, composition theory has moved to embrace postmodern discourse, but composition pedagogy remains unaffected by it. In either case, it is clear that student self-assessment assumes a writer capable of agency, of some sort of independent judgment of self; and it is equally clear that the interrogation of agency that prevails in postmodern theory would ridicule such an assumption. In undertaking something called "self-assessment," we must therefore inquire into the nature of the "self" who will engage in this reflexive assessment.[3] When self-assessment is situated in composition studies, where the modernist self continues to be represented in cognitivist and social constructionist pedagogy, we might expect that the "self" who will "assess" is an autonomous student writer who, as a result of effective composition instruction, can learn to control his or her writing and thereby to assert his or her own identity and change his or her environment. Berlin (1990) offers relief from the quandary when he says that to some, the "loss of the autonomous subject of liberal humanism is . . . the death of the possibility of democratic politics." Berlin says that these fears are answered, however, by Smith's *Discerning the Subject* (1988), which points out that subjects are organized in a "contradictory complex of subject formations" and that negotiation transpires as dialectic, which produces political action and even "a certain conception of individuality and self interest." Because the dialectic takes place in interaction with other subjects, the individual history "is thus situated within a larger social history—the economic, political, and cultural conditions of the time," which allows for individual agency (Berlin, 1990, p. 174).

---

[3]*Self* is another of Freisinger's (1994) "problematic, definitionally complex, and ideologically loaded" terms.

If fresh proposals for self-assessment can achieve a measure of reflexivity—if they can articulate and examine their own underlying assumptions and thereby improve both theory and practice—the field of representation that is student self-assessment may become an important site for easing the tensions that Worsham and Flannery have identified in the discipline. By thematizing the assumptions of the prefix *self* in the label *self-assessment*, the movement has the potential for making these assumptions visible.

In revealing the terms of its own definition, self-assessment has the additional potential for not only revealing but also causing slippage in the dichotomies of composition studies. As I have noted elsewhere (Howard, 1994), we must not assume that we are faced with a binary choice between modernist and postmodern poles. Every binary opposition has in fact a series of points between the poles; and, more interestingly, the interplay between binary oppositions may create one or more other positions that cannot even be located on the continuum that appears to stretch between the poles. It may be, in fact, that "meaning" resides not in any stable "position" but occurs instead in the indeterminacy of process, the fluid dialogue between supposed opposites. Looking for the spaces between and outside binary oppositions takes on a measure of urgency when one recognizes that these oppositions, even when viewed as the poles of a continuum, are seldom imagined on a horizontal axis. Instead they are represented vertically—hierarchically—which privileges one position over another.

In this framework, the movement toward student self-assessment holds out not just the possibility of conducting assessment more equitably or accurately, but of redefining and perhaps replacing the terms of assessment. And in that redefinition and replacement, we may have the opportunity to rub some of the naïveté off the modernist *self* of composition pedagogy by bouncing it against the elusive, deferred self of postmodern composition theory—and in the relays between the two, opening an arena for alternative conceptions of self that are compatible with the desires of composition pedagogy yet capable of validation in *fin-de-millennium* postmodern society.

A second challenge to student self-assessment emerges in the reflexive social science of Bourdieu, who, with Passeron, asserts that the function of education is the reproduction of established power relations. Everyone in the education machine—teachers and students alike—plays his or her part in reproducing and preserving the status quo (Bourdieu & Passeron, 1977/1990). Elsewhere, in *The Forms of Capital*, Bourdieu (1987) appropriates Marxist constructs to assemble his own theoretical apparatus. Economic capital, he says, is the most efficient form of capital, but cultural capital (the stock in trade of educational institutions) functions very powerfully to maintain axes of domination. Cultural capital (a college degree, for example, or placement in an advanced composition course) is attached to the body; it cannot be sold or transferred from the person who has earned it to someone else. Because it is attached to the body, it is often mistaken for a natural aptitude rather than being recognized as an earned commodity. By these means cultural capital operates as a constituent discourse of higher education, specifically in its mission of reproducing and securing established power relations. Because cultural capital is mistaken for natural ability, everyone—student or teacher—plays her or his part in reproducing the system that oppresses (or privileges) the subject. Liberatory pedagogy, then, is an oxymoron: Either the pedagogy will be contradicted and ultimately overpowered by the larger institution in which it takes place, or the liberatory pedagogy will itself unwittingly come to reproduce the status quo, even as it seeks to offer alternatives and to encourage resistance.

No system, however, is infallible. Each has its lacunae, its interstices, its contradictory forces, the places in which it does not function as efficiently as it would wish. It may be possible, therefore, to design student self-assessment to fit into spaces in the educational establishment in which the hegemonic forces of which Bourdieu and Passeron (1977/1990) speak—forces that few theorists would categorically deny—subside. In those spaces, the subject, the student, may be able to exert agency in self-definition, especially if the self is being defined dialogically, in a local context, rather than in the autonomous, hermetic domains postulated by modernism. If the program of self-assessment is well designed, it may encourage the student, in that exercise of agency, to formulate a self-definition that transcends the usual hierarchical rankings occasioned by the prevailing machine of writing assessment—for example, "I'm a 'B' writer"—formulating instead a more dialogic self-image: "I feel confident when writing about poetry, but I haven't studied enough philosophy to be able to understand Langer when I read her works, and so I have difficulty writing about them." One essential component of a dialogic rather than hierarchical self-assessment is the provision of local context, so that the student has recourse not just to context-free, "objective" categories of "ability," but to the context-specific exercise of writing.

ASSESSMENTS MADE OF STUDENTS

The current "machine" of assessment might best be understood in the terms offered by Lucas (1992), the terms of "summative" and "formative" judgments: "In 1967, Scriven coined the term 'summative evaluation' to describe outcomes assessment that yields an external, terminal judgment, as distinct from what he calls 'formative evaluation,' which provides internal, continual feedback to the performer-in-action" (p. 1). Assessment in most of its current manifestations strives to reach summative judgments that will use preexisting categories to hierarchize and label those who are assessed. Most crucially, it also strives for "correct" (read: unassailable) judgments. Summative judgment can be imbedded in both the standardized (norm-referenced) and holistic (criterion-referenced) tests that White (1994) describes. Standardized tests can be machine scored, in a double move that makes standardized testing itself a machine and therefore infallible. In a further complication of the machine of assessment, preparation for holistic testing aims to make a machine of the human testers, giving them common criteria and similar (hence infallible) responses. Often even the physical setting for holistic testing bears eerie resemblance to an industrial factory. The objective of summative testing is control—control in the sense described by Foucault (1979): "Discipline 'makes' individuals; it is the specific technique of a power that regards individuals both as objects and as instruments of its exercise." It utilizes "hierarchical observation, normalizing judgment and their combination in a procedure that is specific to it, the examination" (p. 170). Control is achieved through infallibility; infallibility is achieved through a mechanization that putatively rises above the agendas and quirks of individual humans.

Student self-assessment, in contrast, is customarily used for formative, hence individual, purposes. Proponents of journal-keeping, promoting student self-assessment as a vehicle of learning freed from grade tyranny, have depicted summative and formative judgment as incommensurate, mutually exclusive agendas.[4] Fulwiler's (1989) essay on responding to student journals first talks about formative benefits of and approaches to journals. Only in the closing 2 pages of the 24-page essay does he bring up the issue of grading journals: "I have waited until the end of this chapter to articulate anything approximating 'guidelines' for responding to (or for evaluating) student journal writing" (p. 170). If grades are assigned to journals, Fulwiler says, they should be assigned on the basis of "qualitative features" like personal voice, conversational tone, experimentation and play, emotion, speculation, doubt, questions, self-awareness, connections, digressions, and dialogue, as well as revision.

---

[4] I am not suggesting here that summative evaluation is not intended to benefit the individual; rather, I am establishing a contrast between evaluation that is intended only for immediate, formative benefit to the individual, and that which is intended for the individual's benefit by accurately identifying his or her appropriate place in a hierarchical structure.

Self-evaluation is for Fulwiler a valuable component of learners' journals, and evidence of self-evaluation should increase the grade assigned by the teacher. All of the teacher's grading criteria should promote a dialogic, transactional journal in which learning occurs.

Thomas (1992) explains the importance of teachers' grading: "Most journal advocates agree that students will not take a journal assignment seriously unless it 'counts' for a grade" (p. 10). Because of pressure from students, in other words, the formative self-evaluation in journals must be subordinated to summative judgment—or else the students will resist or sabotage self-assessment. Unlike Fulwiler's (1989) essay, which is devoted to responding to journals and which sees grading them as a potentially competing agenda, Thomas' entire essay addresses the evaluation and grading of journals. After explaining several different ways in which students may evaluate their own essays, however, Thomas makes it clear that it is the teacher, not the student, who assigns the grade.

Anticipating Thomas' (1992) perspective on journals, in 1978 Ford and Larkin touted portfolio evaluation for purposes of summative evaluation, "the best way we know of to combat grade inflation and the decline in students' English abilities" (p. 951). Burnham (1986) also sees summative benefits of portfolio evaluation, in that the system allows inexperienced teachers to develop their grading philosophy and skills in interaction with other teachers. However, as Lucas notes, formative assessment is more commonly associated with portfolio evaluation; Weiser (1992) and Sommers (1991) join her in associating portfolio evaluation with formative rather than summative judgment. Sommers says that portfolio evaluation in all its manifestations strives to free students from "the tyranny of the grade." Larson (1991) also believes that one of the values of portfolios is that they "resist . . . easy summative evaluation" (p. 138).

Although both portfolios and journals have provided models for conducting student self-evaluation for formative purposes, summative judgment still takes place, and typically it is still conducted by the teacher. The teacher still grades the student by employing what Foucault (1979) calls "hierarchical observation [and] normalizing judgment" (p. 170). Self-evaluation is for formative purposes; but the grading, the final decision, is made by the teacher, and with primarily summative outcomes. Those who believe that their grading practices promote formative judgments need only listen to students' self-descriptions—as I did to 61 graduating seniors at a liberal arts college—to learn that they may define themselves as writers almost exclusively by recourse to their grades (R. Howard, 1991).

Yet even as portfolio and journal pedagogies have continued to engage in summative evaluation, they have also revised the terms of summative judgment. In composition pedagogy, summative judgment has traditionally been conducted under the aegis of the transcendent signified of "objective," hierarchized criteria. Portfolio and journal pedagogies have transgressed this tradition by arriving at summative judgment through the application of local criteria that are often developed by the class members as a group and that are often more dialogic than hierarchical. Such innovations complicate dichotomous characterizations of summative judgment as externally imposed, and formative evaluation as limited to learner-internal purposes.

Bullock (1991) further destabilizes the putatively oppositional relationship between summative and formative when he advocates that students be involved in self-assessment for purposes of summative judgment, participating in determining their course grades. Nor is he alone in this proposition: Beaven (1977) advocates making students' grading of their own work a part of self-assessment, and she notes that 90% of the grades the students gave themselves correlated with the grades she would have given them. Bullock describes student participation in course grading as a curative for standardized testing, which reifies "something called 'writing ability' that can be measured in individuals and compared across large populations, rather than seeing these students as 'webs of contingency,' individual and unique, with their own stories to tell (and retell)" (p. 198). He offers a hypothetical scenario, however, that addresses not course placement but how grades within a course are determined.

ABILITY GROUPING

Student self-assessment has a potentially valuable role not just in determining grades for a course but also in course placement, where it not only can occur prior to summative assessment but can also become the means for it. The institution of such a change, however, requires the dismantling of a long-established practice known variously as *ability grouping* or *tracking*. Colleges test and label students' writing ability. According to that label they determine who must take a composition course, and what kind of course they will be required to take. Colleges also stratify composition instruction, designating some courses as more "advanced" than others, appropriate to students at a certain level of labeled "ability"—a sort of curricular food chain. Often all three means of ability grouping are employed at a single institution, where students are first labeled according to ability and then sorted and assigned to a certain "level" of composition course whose instruction corresponds to their identified ability.

Ability grouping prevails in higher education because it seems to proceed on a "natural" rationale. A linchpin in that rationale is the belief in a hierarchy of writing skills. Warfel declared in 1955, "Expertness in writing the simple sentence patterns must be achieved first, and then the many ways of saying anything can be added as occasion warrants" (cited in Berlin, 1987, p. 113). This vision of writing supports not only ability grouping but also bottom-to-top pedagogy, which teaches the mechanics first, then sentence structure, then paragraph development, then the essay. Ability grouping and bottom-to-top pedagogy participate in the same cultural logistics: writing skills and students' abilities are hierarchically arranged and should be addressed in hierarchical sequence.

Dillon (1991) has effectively challenged the "bottom-to-top" rhetoric (and pedagogy) that assumes readers (and writers) build meaning first through grammar, then sentence structure, then paragraphs, then essays. However, whereas bottom-to-top pedagogy has waned as a model for college composition instruction, the constituent discourse of ability grouping has until very recently still been seen as a "natural" way to determine who gets what instruction.

As Huot's (1994) survey demonstrates, many colleges, notwithstanding the efforts of scholars like White (1994), still ascertain "writing ability" according to students' scores on standardized tests that measure facility with the prestige variety variously known as "standard English," "good English," or "correct English." The machine scoring of these tests, mechanized and therefore beyond error, establishes Standard Written English not only as a norm but also as a transcendent signified, a determinate touchstone for contiguous, indeterminate formations such as writing itself.

Using such tests for composition placement makes *writing ability* a trope for facility with the standard—which in turn readily serves as a trope for social class difference, because the dialects of various social groups differentially resemble the standard and because the degree to which the dialect of a given social group approximates the standard correlates with the social prestige of that group. Many critics of ability grouping—both scholars (see, for example, Ball, 1981, and Oakes, 1988) and policy makers (see "Governors," 1990)—charge the practice with reproducing social inequality by placing students of color and those of low social class in remedial writing courses, which defines them as nonparticipants in academic literacy—and in turn limits their ability to imagine themselves as participants and thus to act on that imagining. Significantly, for these commentators it is not a question of what type of test determines ability grouping; it is the practice of ability grouping itself that is the culprit.

Part of its culpability is its denial of context. Ability grouping asserts that writers possess context-free "skills" and "abilities" and that they move through generic, predictable, measurable stages of intellectual and rhetorical development. This assertion contradicts fundamental principles of writing across the curriculum (or more specifically, writing in the disciplines): that writing is specific to contexts and that writing "abilities" in one context may not translate readily to writing success in another. Social constructionism, too, pulls against ability grouping by depicting writing "abilities" as a product not of learner-internal development but of learner-external social forces, the writer's places in his or her various communities.

The crux of the problem with ability grouping is that it is predicated on a false yet pervasive notion of cultural capital. It is at this juncture that Bourdieu's (1987) theories come to the fore: He describes education as cultural capital acquired slowly and laboriously. One person cannot acquire an education (which would include acquiring facility with the standard dialect) and then transfer that capital to another person, except insofar as the second person, also undertakes the slow, laborious course of study that results in the cultural capital of education. Cultural capital cannot be transferred from one person to another because it is attached to the body of the person who earns it. Yet in its attachment to the body, cultural capital tends to masquerade as "legitimate competence" rather than as an earned asset. When cultural capital translates into the academic success that grades (including grades on writing placement exams) intend to measure, the commonsense view depicts it as a "natural aptitude."

Thus ability assumes the same role that Gates (1986) attributes to the word *race*: It becomes a trope for "irreducible difference," and that irreducible difference is "between cultures, linguistic groups, or adherents of specific belief systems which—more often than not—also have fundamentally opposed economic interests" (p. 5). That the cultural capital of grades on writing placement exams is believed to represent "natural aptitude" is evidenced in our culture's dominant metaphor for remedial or developmental composition: *bonehead English*, a term always spoken with a sheepish grin, a term that serves as a relay point between ability grouping and natural aptitude—the association with the body. The bodies that it identifies are those of the masses, the Great Unwashed, from whom, Carey explains, the intelligentsia was endeavoring to differentiate itself at the end of the 19th century—at approximately the same time that composition instruction and ability grouping were born (Berlin, 1987), each parented by a need to bring the newly educated children of the middle and sometimes lower classes to approximate the speech and manners (if not the intellect) of the traditionally privileged (Berlin, 1987; Lunsford, 1991).[5]

These cultural logistics have become sufficiently visible that ability grouping is now under challenge and on the wane. As McCleary (1990) details, ability grouping has come to be seen as a means whereby socially stratified groups are kept apart rather than brought together; and insofar as ability grouping accomplishes the erasure of difference, it does so at the expense of the language, rhetoric, and values of subordinate groups. Like the Advanced Placement described by Ohmann (1976), it "domesticates" all whom it touches. Ability grouping has fallen sufficiently far from favor that the National Governors' Association in 1990 called for the end of "segregating students by ability" ("Governors," 1990).

MIXED-ABILITY INSTRUCTION

Those who would implement student self-assessment as a component of composition course placement must therefore first unseat ability grouping as the "natural" and necessary practice, which entails challenging the very notion of a context-free writing "ability." As they undertook curriculum revision in 1986, the Writing faculty at my university resolved to design course offerings that would not reproduce social difference, a resolution that led to rejecting ability grouping as a principle for structuring the composition curriculum. In the "inevitable historical flux" that Elbow and Belanoff (1991) attribute to developing pedagogical practices, our first solution was a mixed-ability curriculum. (Only later, when the shortcomings of mixed-ability curricula became evident, did the trope of writing ability become visible. And only then did student self-assessment emerge as an alternative to both ability grouping and mixed-ability instruction.)

Even while instituting a curriculum consisting of mixed-ability classes, the Writing faculty voted to continue requiring some students to take Composition based on their standardized test scores—a practice that White (1994) and others identify as one of the least accurate means available and which Bullock and others believe reinforces social difference. The metaphor of context-free, hierarchized writing ability exerts a strong pull even on those who are consciously trying to escape it.

---

[5]Berlin (1987) describes the emergence of ability grouping in the early years of composition curricula. Berlin, Lunsford (1991), and Ohmann (1976) are three very different sources providing texture to the intellectual class agenda that propelled the focus on "correct English."

The composition courses in the new mixed-ability curriculum were topically rather than hierarchically arranged, and students were free to choose among them. Some options were writing-across-the-curriculum courses such as "Social Darwinism" (taught by an historian) and "Reproductive Issues" (taught by a biologist). Some were half-credit "writing segments" linked to other courses in the university curriculum. Still others were writing segments that focused on (but were not limited to) certain phases or components of the writing process, such as writing with word processing, sentence style, or grammar and mechanics.

These mixed-ability classes had distinct advantages. Students could select courses on topics that actually interested them—which increased their willingness to engage the course materials. Once in the class, peer response pedagogy encouraged them to realize that all writers can learn from one another, regardless of their "level." Student writers who had been required to take composition might realize that they knew something about writing that they could share with their classmates. Conversely, those who had not been required to take composition but who nevertheless chose to do so might realize that they had things to learn not just from an authoritative teacher, but from their classmates, as well. *All* of their classmates. The courses spoke to the similarities between writers: Course selection brought together people with common interests, regardless of any judgment that standardized testing may have made of their "writing ability." The absence of levels of instruction (developmental-introductory-advanced) reduced both the stigma attached to students who were required to take composition (approximately 20% of the student population at the university) and the self-fulfilling prophecies that so often result from that stigma. From the teachers' point of view, the curriculum was stimulating because it prevented them from beginning a class with preconceived notions (read: stereotypes) about their students' needs. Instead, they had to devise pedagogy that responded to the real needs of the individual students in any given class.

Mixed-ability instruction had its shortcomings, however, and these, too, were substantial. One of these was the staffing problems created by exceptionally small class size: Mixed-ability groups unavoidably press the teacher into increased one-on-one work, instruction individualized to the various members of the class. Sometimes a composition section would evolve into entirely one-to-one pedagogy, because the needs of the students were so diverse. Although one-to-one pedagogy has its unassailable benefits, when it becomes the sole or even dominant pedagogy, the teacher's workload increases and class sizes must commensurably decrease. Moreover, exclusive or dominant one-to-one pedagogy preempted the mixed-ability dialogue that the curriculum was designed to foster. And, crucially, as the 1990s brought increased financial pressure to higher education, the exceptionally small class sizes necessitated by mixed-ability pedagogy became a luxury the university could ill afford.

What prompted the search for alternatives to mixed-ability instruction, however, was not economic pressure as much as the social problems encountered in the classroom. However vigorously teachers may assert the fallacies of ability grouping, students come to college interpellated by an educational lifetime of summative evaluation. They know their scores, they know their grades, they believe that these measure their "abilities," and they want their abilities to be acknowledged and improved. Those who have been labeled as weak writers sometimes want to contest these labels and insist that they should not, in fact, be required to take composition. For them, composition instruction is a badge of dishonor, one that they have to resist in order to preserve their good names. To accept instruction in composition is tantamount to acknowledging that they are, indeed, boneheads. Forced into these classes, they therefore spend their energy in demonstrating—and sometimes aggressively asserting—that composition instruction is beneath them. Students who have been certified as capable writers but who nevertheless choose to enroll in composition also have problems with mixed-ability instruction. Carrying the notion of "ability level" into a mixed-ability classroom, they find themselves among classmates with more nonstandard usage than they, and they therefore conclude that these "error makers" are of lesser "ability" than they—and that it was a mistake to have signed up for this class. Still others, regardless of whether their labeling was negative or positive, have very little confidence in their writing and feel intimidated by their more confident classmates. These students long for a class that is geared to their particular needs, their lack of confidence, their supposed lack of ability.

In sum, the greatest impediment to mixed-ability instruction is students' attitudes. Just as Bourdieu and Passeron (1977/1990) assert, students have been interpellated by their education: They believe in ability levels, and many of them feel uncomfortable in a curriculum that does not respond to their beliefs about writing and writing instruction. In the mixed-ability instruction at my university, too much of the teachers' instructional time was squandered in fruitless attempts to change these attitudes.

ASSESSMENTS MADE BY STUDENTS

A rejection of both ability grouping and mixed-ability instruction prompts an inquiry into whether "ability" is the only way to sort writers. Even the theorists who oppose ability grouping may nevertheless subscribe to the notion of ability: Ball, (1981), for example, proposes "mixed-ability" curricula as an alternative to ability grouping. Our mixed-ability curriculum had done the same. Dissatisfied with the results, as the curriculum specialist in my department I found myself questioning the trope of ability that underlies both ability grouping and mixed-ability instruction. However, I had to take into account how powerfully and intractably that trope makes meaning for the students who come to composition classes—especially when the university, also in the sway of the trope, has used standardized tests to determine whether students' enrollment in composition shall be compulsory.

In the second wave of our "inevitable historical flux" away from ability grouping, a pilot project therefore sorted composition students not according to their ability or their interests, but their self-image. This self-image, moreover, was not something that was determined about the students, but something that they were asked to determine about themselves. The pilot project undertook to involve the students in self-assessment for summative purposes, opening up a new range of possibility for student self-assessment.

The pilot project was instituted in a 1992 Colgate University summer program designed for underprepared students who in the fall would begin their first year at the university. Although Colgate is a liberal-arts college that describes itself as "competitive" and although its student population consists of a larger number of well-prepared students than characterize most other American institutions, it nevertheless has an appreciable population of underprepared—and sometimes profoundly underprepared—students whose instructional needs must be addressed. For some of the underprepared, this summer program addresses those needs.

One of the premises of the pilot project was that teaching must begin where the students are. "Where they are" is firmly entrenched in the hierarchy that a schooling lifetime of ability grouping has taught them is natural. Instead of challenging that trope, the pilot placement system sounded reassuringly like what they were accustomed to. The difference was that the self-assessment was made not according to ability but according to how well prepared for college writing the students believed themselves—a sort of self-image self-tracking. As they made their self-assessments, the students knew that they would be placed in summer composition courses with peers of similar self-perceptions and that the writing instruction would be tailored to the needs of the group. As Figure 3.1 demonstrates, the questionnaire for this pilot project of self-assessment was of the utmost simplicity.

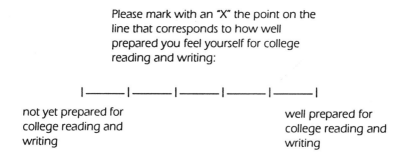

Please mark with an "X" the point on the line that corresponds to how well prepared you feel yourself for college reading and writing:

|——|——|——|——|——|

not yet prepared for college reading and writing

well prepared for college reading and writing

Figure 3.1. Self-assessment instrument (first version)

The ensuing 2 years of self-image self-tracking satisfied everyone. Administrators in charge of the summer program observed that, for the first time in living memory, no students complained that they should not have been required to take composition. In previous summers of mixed-ability instruction, some students—predictably those coming from prep schools or prestigious high schools—had protested that they "did not need" composition instruction. These protests simply ceased—utterly ceased—in the curriculum of self-image self-tracking. Nor did any believe themselves misplaced (a common complaint in programs based on ability grouping), because they had placed themselves. All of the students believed they had received appropriate composition instruction. Teachers also like the arrangement. Both Vicky McMillan and Margaret Darby (personal communication, August, 1993) observed no palpable classroom effects of self-image self-tracking— except the absence of the classroom problems that usually arise in ability grouped or mixed-ability classes.

Tom Howard (personal communication, July, 1994), who has taught in all three types of curricula, was specific about the potential negative effects of the alternative curricular arrangements: He recalled a mixed-ability class in which students jockeyed to establish themselves as the superior writers, and an ability-grouped curriculum in which students strove to "move up" as quickly as possible. "It was dog eat dog," he said. Again, the curricular food chain.

What is remarkable about self-image self-tracking, T. Howard said, is an absence—the absence of contention among students. They share a self-perception of themselves as writers, and they share a sense of common purpose. Sandra Jamieson, who has taught the low-self-esteem group in self-image self-tracking as well as the bottom group in ability grouping, believes that it is in the low group that self-image self-tracking matters most. In an ability-grouped low group, she says that some students believe themselves to be misplaced and therefore resist instruction, whereas in the low group of self-image self-tracking, a sense of common purpose and mutual support prevails. No one derides anyone else.

Robert Osgood (personal communication, July, 1994), who taught a middle group of self-image self-tracked students, found no trace in their journals of resentment or discomfort. Nor does he think that his students were particularly aware of or interested in the means by which they were placed in his class. He believes that the most profound influence of self-image self-tracking is within himself as a teacher. Because he knew that his students were of average self-esteem, he is careful to respond to their writing in ways that would build that self-esteem.

However, all these positive instrumental outcomes are insufficient. A reflexive examination of the assumptions underlying self-image self-tracking raises questions about the "self" postulated by this curriculum. Because the students in the first two years of the pilot program were asked the simple question, "Please mark with an "X" the point on the line that corresponds to how well prepared you feel yourself for college reading and writing," that self might very easily be the hierarchically situated self produced by their 12 years of ability grouping and capped by the summative evaluations that had placed them in this developmental summer program. Asked the context-free question about their preparedness for college writing, they might very well call upon their beliefs about their writing ability and use that as the yardstick for making an "X" at a point on the line. What the placement instrument may have done, therefore, is call on the trope of ability, asking the students to play their own part—as Bourdieu and Passeron (1977/1990) would have it—in reproducing the power relations of the academy.

The third year of the self-tracked summer program therefore employed a revised placement instrument that situated students' self-assessment in the local context of required General Education courses at the university. The placement instrument is less simplistic, for it provides a sample writing assignment given in a General Education course for first-year students, together with two-page excerpts from two assigned readings (see Figure 3.2).

Dear,

One of the courses you will be taking this summer will be a composition course called "Critical Reading and Writing" that is designed to prepare you for successful work in Colgate courses this fall. So that we can place you in a composition course suited to your needs, we ask that you fill out the attached sheet, describing how well prepared you feel for reading and writing at Colgate. You will then be placed in a composition course with students who feel themselves similarly prepared, and the instruction of that course will be tailored to the needs of its students.

To help you decide how prepared you are for work at Colgate, I am enclosing (1) sample passages from assigned readings in two courses required of all first- and second-year Colgate students, General Education 101 and 102; and (2) sample writing assignments given in those courses. You can look these materials over, compare them with your reading and writing experiences and instruction in high school, and then fill out the attached questionnaire and return it so that we can place you in an appropriate section of Critical Reading and Writing.

The summer program composition faculty look forward to your arrival and to helping you prepare for successful academic experiences in the fall term.

Figure 3.2. Letter inviting self-assessment

Students are then asked to describe how well prepared they are for reading and writing at this university and to make these judgments about reading and writing as separate tasks (see Figure 3.3).

Although their beliefs about their abstract writing abilities may still play a role in the students' self-assessments, this instrument encourages a dialogic rather than hierarchical judgment. As the cover letter in Figure 3.2 indicates, the students are invited to put their past and prospective literacy experiences in interaction and to imagine the relative difficulty or ease with which they will negotiate the intervening terrain. Nietzsche (1967) suggests that the "doer" is a "fiction"; that there is nothing but the deed. The self-assessment in which these students are engaged does not ask them to assess that fictional doer, the self, in isolation, but to think of that self in terms of deeds—the deeds of past and future writing instruction and experiences—and to imagine the relative difficulty or ease with which they will accomplish those deeds. This is a self that makes sense in a *fin-de-millennium* composition curriculum. It postulates composition pedagogy as a means neither for liberating students from the confines of a hierarchizing institution—for, as Russell (1993) and many others have observed, there is no "outside"

By June 10, 1994, please fill out this sheet, place it in the enclosed envelope, and return it to the Office of Undergraduate Studies.

Name (please print):_____

Date:_____

Please mark with an "X" the point on the line that corresponds to how well prepared you feel yourself for reading at Colgate:

I———I———I———I———I———I

not yet prepared for   well prepared for
Colgate reading   Colgate reading

Please use this space for any comments you might wish to make about how prepared you are for college reading:

Please mark with an "X" the point on the line that corresponds to how well prepared you feel yourself for writing at Colgate:

I———I———I———I———I———I

not yet prepared for   well prepared for
Colgate writing   Colgate writing

Please use this space for any comments you might wish to make about how prepared you are for college writing:

Figure 3.3. Self-assessment instrument (revised version)

natural world to which one can escape—nor for inscribing them in that hierarchy. Instead, it revises the hierarchy, creating a type of tracking that involves individual choice and individual agency. Like most composition practices, it affirms the possibility of individual choice and agency; but it does so while recognizing that these constructs are socially produced and while thus endeavoring to make that production a positive dialogue rather than a limiting hierarchization.

The successful pilot developmental summer program of self-image self-tracking has provided a guiding structure for a subsequent complete revision of the regular composition curriculum at the university. Although the principle of offering students a choice among many topics and modes of instruction remained, the entire curriculum of mixed-ability instruction gave way to a hierarchized curriculum of introductory, intermediate, and advanced composition courses. Those students who are required to take composition can choose from any full-credit course on the introductory or intermediate level. Thus they still have many possibilities from which to choose, and these possibilities now include multiple levels of instruction, so that students will no longer feel that their composition instruction is in conflict with what they perceive as their abilities and corollary needs. An as-yet-unresolved question is whether students will continue to be required to take composition based on standardized testing; whether it will be replaced by the more respectable holistic evaluation; or whether student self-assessment will constitute not just the second stage of, but the entire mechanism for, composition course placement.

REFERENCES

Ball, S. J. (1981). *Beachside comprehensive*. London: Cambridge University Press.

Bazerman, C. (1992). The interpretation of disciplinary writing. In R.H. Brown (Ed.), *Writing the social text: Poetics and politics in social science discourse* (pp. 31-33). New York: Aldine de Gruyter.

Beach, R. (1976). Self-evaluation strategies of extensive revisers and non-revisers. *College Composition and Communication, 27*, 160-64.

Beach, R. (1989). Showing students how to assess: Demonstrating techniques for response in the writing conference. In C.M. Anson (Ed.), *Writing and response: Theory, practice, and research* (pp. 127-148). Urbana, IL: National Council of Teachers of English.

Beaven, M. H. (1977). Individualized goal setting, self-evaluation, and peer evaluation. In C. R. Cooper & L. Odell (Eds.), *Evaluating writing* (pp. 135-153). Urbana, IL: National Council of Teachers of English.

Berlin, J. A. (1987). *Rhetoric and reality: Writing instruction in American colleges, 1900-1985.* Carbondale: Southern Illinois University Press.

Berlin, J. A. (1990, Fall/Winter). Postmodernism, politics, and histories of rhetoric. *Pre/Text, 11*(3-4), 169-188.

Bourdieu, P. (1987). The forms of capital. In J. G. Richardson (Ed.), *Handbook of theory and research for the sociology of education* (pp. 241–258). Westport, CT: Greenwood.

Bourdieu, P., & Passeron, J.-C. (1990). *Reproduction in education, society and culture.* Newbury Park, CA: Sage. (Original work published 1977)

Bullock, R. (1991). Autonomy and community in the evaluation of writing. In R. Bullock & J. Trimbur (Eds.), *The politics of writing instruction: Postsecondary* (pp. 189–202). Portsmouth, NH: Boynton/Cook.

Burnham, C. C. (1986). Portfolio evaluation: Room to breathe and grow. In C. W. Bridges (Ed.), *Training the new teacher of college composition* (pp. 125–138). Urbana, IL: National Council of Teachers of English.

Carey, J. (1992). *The intellectuals and the masses: Pride and prejudice among the literary intelligentsia, 1880-1939.* New York: St. Martin's Press.

Dillon, G. (1981). *Constructing texts: Elements of a theory of composition and style.* Bloomington: Indiana University Press.

Elbow, P., & Belanoff, P. (1991). State University of New York at Stony Brook portfolio-based evaluation program. In P. Belanoff & M. Dickson (Eds.), *Portfolios: Process and product* (pp. 3–16). Portsmouth, NH: Boynton/Cook.

Flannery, K. T. (1991, October). Composing and the question of agency. *College English, 53*(6), 701-713.

Ford, J. E., & Larkin, G. (1978). The portfolio system: An end to backsliding writing standards. *College English, 39,* 950-955.

Foucault, M. (1979). *Discipline and punish: The birth of the prison* (A. Sheridan, Trans.). New York: Vintage.

Freisinger, R. R. (1994). Voicing the self: Toward a pedagogy of resistance in a postmodern age. In K. B. Yancey (Ed.), *Voices on voice: Definitions, perspectives, inquiry* (pp. 242–274). Urbana, IL: National Council of Teachers of English.

Fulwiler, T. (1989). Responding to student journals. In C. M. Anson (Ed.), *Writing and response: Theory, practice, and research* (pp. 149–173). Urbana, IL: National Council of Teachers of English.

Gates, H. L., Jr. (Ed.). (1986). *"Race," writing, and difference.* Chicago: University of Chicago Press.

Governors pushing education issue. (1990, July 29). *New York Times,* p. A22.

Howard, R. M. (1991, December). *The hierarchical construction of undergraduate writers.* Paper presented at the meeting of the Modern Language Association, San Francisco, CA.

Howard, R. M. (1994, March). Reflexivity and agency in rhetoric and pedagogy. *College English, 56*(3), 348-355.

Huot, B. (1994, Spring). A survey of college and university writing placement practices. *WPA: Writing Program Administration, 17*(3), 49-65.

Larson, R. L. (1991). Using portfolios in the assessment of writing in the academic disciplines. In P. Belanoff & M. Dickson (Eds.), *Portfolios: Process and product* (pp. 137–149). Portsmouth, NH: Boynton/Cook.

Lucas, C. (1992). Writing portfolios—Changes and challenges. In K. B. Yancey (Ed.), *Portfolios in the writing classroom: An introduction* (pp. 1–11). Urbana, IL: National Council of Teachers of English.

Lunsford, A. (1991). The nature of composition studies. In E. Lindemann & G. Tate (Eds.), *An introduction to composition studies* (pp. 3–14). New York: Oxford University Press.

McCarthy, P., Meier, S., & Rinderer, R. (1985, December). Self-efficacy and writing: A different view of self-evaluation. *College Composition and Communication, 36*(4), 465-471.

McCleary, B. (1990, February). "Action plan for the education of minorities" implies challenges for English teachers. *Composition Chronicle, 3*, 1-2.

Nietzsche, F. (1967). *On the genealogy of morals* (W. Kaufmann & R. J. Hollingdale, Trans.). New York: Vintage.

Oakes, J. (1988). Tracking in mathematics and science education: A structural contribution to unequal schooling. In L. Weis (Ed.), *Class, race, and gender in American education* (pp. 106–125) Albany: State University of New York Press.

Ohmann, R. (1976). *English in America.* New York: Oxford University Press.

Russell, D. R. (1993, Winter). Vygotsky, Dewey, and externalism: Beyond the student/discipline dichotomy. *Journal of Advanced Composition, 13*(1), 173-198.

Smith, P. (1988). *Discerning the subject.* Minneapolis: University of Minnesota Press.

Sommers, J. (1991). Bringing practice in line with theory: Using portfolio grading in the composition classroom. In P. Belanoff & M. Dickson (Eds.), *Portfolios: Process and product* (pp. 153–164). Portsmouth, NH: Boynton/Cook.

Thomas, T. (1992, Fall). Restless minds take stock: Self-evaluation of student journals. *ATAC Forum, 4*(2), 10-16.

Weiser, I. (1992). Portfolio practice and assessment for collegiate basic writers. In K. B. Yancey, (Ed.), *Portfolios in the writing classroom: An introduction* (pp. 1–11). Urbana, IL: National Council of Teachers of English.

White, E. M. (1994). *Teaching and assessing writing* (2nd ed.). San Francisco: Jossey-Bass.

Worsham, L. (1991). Writing against writing: The predicament of *écriture féminine* in composition studies. In P. Harkin & J. Schilb (Eds.), *Contending with words: Composition and rhetoric in a postmodern age* (pp. 82–104). New York: Modern Language Association.

Yancey, K. B., & Spooner. M. (1994). Concluding the text: Notes toward a theory and the practice of voice. In K. B. Yancey (Ed.), *Voices on voice: Definitions, perspectives, inquiry* (pp. 298-314). Urbana: National Council of Teachers of English.

4

TALKING ABOUT WRITING: A CLASSROOM-BASED STUDY OF STUDENTS' REFLECTIONS ON THEIR DRAFTS

Chris M. Anson

North Carolina State University

Bruce, an experienced, published writer, is reflecting on an article he has drafted for a newsletter circulated among the teachers and parents at his children's elementary school. The newsletter's editor has asked him to write a brief, informative piece focusing on how the school builds conflict resolution into its elementary curriculum. Here is an excerpt of Bruce's tape-recorded discussion of his rough draft:

> *I'm having a harder time writing this than much, than many things I write, and, and that's odd because this is a warm, friendly sort of community. I think it's because, it might be because I'm trying to be sort of punchy, maybe witty, to kind of lighten the thing up. I mean, conflict resolution, conflicts are problems, so you begin reading anything on that with a negative feeling. But the school, the program there is really unique, and I learned so much interviewing the teachers about what they do. So I started out with the adult world, with how huge some problems seem to kids, you know, a stolen toy I likened to grand larceny, a small push is like assault with intent to kill. Then led in to the idea in the third paragraph that even though these conflicts seem small to adults, if, we need to show kids how to deal with them so that when they do face major, the major problems of the adult world, they'll have the right strategies. I need to work some more on, uh, trying, on get—weaving the interview material more effectively into the exposition, and also on the, the conclusion strikes me as almost too much like a PR thing on the school, too much advocacy. That's gonna be hard because I feel strongly about what the school, about the methods. And so my roles, writer, parent, objective volunteer-reporter, are sticky.*

Terry, a first-year college student enrolled in a standard required composition course, is writing a paper based on a personal experience. Terry has been struggling in the course, barely able to maintain a "C" average. He has told his teacher that he has never been a very successful writer and doesn't enjoy writing. Here is Terry's tape-recorded discussion of his rough draft:

> *Ok, I'll go over the paper a little bit. The beginning's just kind of sketchy right now; it's just kind of a basic introduction. Then, from then on, it's going OK; it still needs some work, though. I gotta rearrange some stuff around. I'm trying to put in a couple of analogies in there, because I like writers that can use analogies real good in their writing. Everything's going pretty good with it except it's the old problem of me writing too slow. I just can't flow when I write . . . it's not so much writer's block, it's that I just try to think about what I write too much.*

What strikes us immediately about the difference between Bruce and Terry's descriptions is how they *represent* writing—as a process, as a socially constructed and mediated activity, and as an inscription of their authorial roles. Immersed in his ideas, Bruce talks fluidly; he is projective, hesitant, but in control of his emerging text. In contrast, Terry's metacommentary reveals a writer almost ashamed of his own uncertainty, unable or perhaps unwilling to talk with much specificity about his paper. Whereas Bruce is conscious of his intended readers and the social context of his prose, Terry appears locked into his own awkward relationship with his writing, a relationship constructed from social stereotypes of "style" and misconceptions about the way good writers work (with a constant "flow" that comes from not having to think much about what they want to say). As Bruce unravels his multiple personae and considers their manifestation in his emerging text, Terry struggles with his relationship to his writing, now painfully disclosing its limitations, now repairing the damage with half-hearted authorial assurance: It's going OK; everything's going pretty good.

In the past, comparisons of proficient writers like Bruce with novice writers like Terry focused predominantly on the kinds of texts they wrote. Good writers like Bruce create more stylized, balanced, structured, readable, correct, and "intelligent" texts, whereas struggling writers like Terry produce writing that is difficult to read, filled with errors, unstructured, unpolished, and unsophisticated. Interest in cognitive studies throughout the 1980s began to examine what writers do as they write. However, very little research in composition studies asked about the ways in which writers represent their own writing processes—how they talk *about* their writing.

The idea of exploring writers' reflections on their emerging texts has important implications for our understanding of how writers develop expertise. For example, if we were to find consistent differences in novice and experienced writers' representations of their own work, we might be able to derive some principles of growth that could be useful for instructional practice. Interested in this question, I set out to conduct a series of purely descriptive, classroom-based investigations of how young, inexperienced writers talk about their writing after they have produced a full rough draft of an essay. My goal was mainly local and personal, as is often the case in classroom-based research: I wanted to help my students to improve their own sense of themselves as writers, and I wanted to do so from a more informed position. Over time, I found that these descriptive studies changed much of what I now do in the composition classroom.

TAPED ACCOUNTS OF IN-PROGRESS DRAFTS

Most people can drive a car successfully even though they are not always aware of everything they are doing. A driver can downshift into third gear, make a turn, fiddle with the radio to tune in a station, and glance in the rearview mirror to see if a car is still following too closely, all while attending to a point being made by someone on the carphone. In juggling these simultaneous processes, the driver must allocate attention to some behaviors while letting others fade into the background of thought.

In his important work on the psychology of learning, Polanyi (1966) describes these aspects of thought as *focal* and *tacit*. When we write, Polanyi implies, some of what happens in our minds is focal—we are aware of attending to a problem, making a decision, or needing to return to our work with more information. We can talk about focal knowledge because it is mostly conscious. A writer is aware of wrestling with a particular textual decision because of the time it takes to consider the options and, in a handwritten draft, because of the visual record left behind.

In contrast, tacit knowledge is mostly unconscious, as the term implies. In writing, we make certain choices without being aware of why we are making them, usually because we are too busy attending to focal concerns. Because writing involves so many simultaneous decisions and strategies, we can attend only to those that, at the time, seem most important. When we revise, many of our tacitly made choices emerge into consciousness for our (re)consideration. Writers who take their drafts through multiple revisions exploit the opportunity to keep cycling through their work in search of textual choices or ideas that can be consciously scrutinized.

The relationship between these two kinds of knowledge in the writing process is at best murky. It does not seem likely that writers are entirely aware of all focal decisions and entirely unconscious of tacitly made decisions, only that the latter take a back seat to the former, which at the moment require more deliberate attention and manipulation. Nor does it appear that tacit knowledge is unavailable for retrieval; several studies, for example, show that when writers are asked to discuss specific aspects of their texts retrospectively, they often explain and justify their choices by referring to their purposes, audiences, and other social and pragmatic dimensions of their writing (e.g., Odell, Goswami, & Herrington, 1983; Odell, Goswami, & Quick, 1983). However, this research also suggests that the writers make many of their decisions without paying conscious attention to them at the time of composing. For example, when asked why she addressed a memo "Dear Susan" instead of "Dear Ms. Smith," a business writer may explain in detail her professional relationship with Susan, the level of formality she has established with Susan, the nature of the memo and its requirements, and the presence or absence of copies to other readers. At the time of writing, however, she may have written "Dear Susan" while thinking consciously about something else—for example, worrying about whether to copy the memo to Susan's supervisor.

Composing-aloud protocols such as those used by Emig (1971) and Flower and Hayes (1977, 1980, 1981) tap into writers' focal knowledge by recording the moment-by-moment decisions of writers at work. Because they are actually at work on their prose, writers cannot attend to their tacit decisions unless they go back over their drafts at a later time and rework them. The strength of composing aloud lies in the directness of the data it provides; however, it is limited in not allowing us to listen to the writer once he or she has disengaged from the very demanding task of putting words on a page—a task that in itself may be "intruded upon" by the additional demands of simultaneously talking about it (see Rose, 1980).

If composing aloud reflects the "live" or "concurrent" processes of writing (Smagorinsky, 1989), retrospective accounts (after-the-fact descriptions of what happened) draw out writers' memories of the writing event. In giving such accounts, writers are asked to recall what they did in producing a piece of writing—how they started, where they got stuck, or what they were concerned about as they wrote. In contrast to composing-aloud data, retrospective accounts also allow writers opportunities to uncover tacit decisions as well as focal ones. The process of standing outside their writing, looking it over, recalling what they did when they composed it, and thinking about what else they need to do taps into both the conscious creation and manipulation of text and what may have been, at the time, decisions made in the background of their attention. The result is a representation, or model, of writing.

Retrospective accounts have been critiqued in numerous essays in the field of psychology as well as in composition studies (for various discussions, see Ericsson & Simon, 1980, 1984; Smagorinsky, 1989; Steinberg, 1986; Tomlinson, 1984). For example, they are said to be influenced by the subject's memory limitations, the possible intrusion of an experimenter's "prompts" in the writer's recall, and the tendency for subjects to embellish (knowingly nor not) what was really happening to them during the event being recalled. In her discussion of these limitations, Tomlinson (1984) has noted that although such accounts may not be useful in trying to understand precisely what happens during the writing process, they show us the writer's representation of the writing event and its context. As people write, in other words, they are drawing on the same ways of thinking *about* writing as when they later talk about what they have done.

In providing "narratives" about a writer's creation of a text, retrospective accounts give us insight into the writer's knowledge, modes of inquiry, relationship to the text, social construction of an audience, stance, role, and routines (Finley, 1995). As Carter (1993) has suggested, narratives of experience are part of human cognition: "The mind is constantly building models . . . and stories are at the center of this constructive process. To understand thinking, it is necessary to find the story that structures an individual's model of theory and events" (p. 7).

A CLASSROOM-BASED STUDY OF REFLECTIVE METACOMMENTARY

An important limitation of clinically based studies of writing, particularly cognitively-based studies using composing-aloud protocols, concerns the writer's context. Writers working in "experimental" settings are no doubt influenced by their interpretation of the researcher's goals, the atypical or unrealistic setting in which they are placed, and the fact that their writing may have no audience or purpose beyond the experiment (see Berkenkotter, 1983). For this reason, I chose to look at the ways in which students talk about their writing in the context of actual instructional settings.

In keeping with more naturalistic studies of writing, the "data"— narrative commentaries about the process of writing a first draft—were part of the structure and expectations of the courses. In each course, I asked students to provide me with a brief, tape-recorded account of their in-progress first drafts of papers, along with the drafts, so that I could respond more sensitively to their needs. Interested in how students talked about their writing, I offered them few strict guidelines about the focus of their tapes. The tapes were designed to help me understand their concerns as writers. As such, they had a strong retrospective quality: The drafts had already been written, and the writers were reflecting on their experiences to that point in time. However, many of the commentaries also looked ahead to a finished text. The accounts, therefore, are more reflective than purely retrospective.

In each class in which I used this method, I duplicated the tapes for later analysis and transcription. In all cases, students provided releases for the use of the tapes at the end of the course. As in much classroom-based research, I was also aware of students' performance as writers from a wealth of sources, primarily the evolution of their work during the course. In this way, I could study carefully the tapes of students with different levels of ability as writers, as well as any changes in the nature of the students' talk as they developed greater expertise.

In early analyses of the taped accounts, I was chiefly interested in the focus of students' comments. In some cases, the students seemed unable or reluctant to talk about their writing very deliberately or with much attention to its ideas, structure, or purposes. Instead, they offered short, somewhat hesitant assessments of the writing, often confessing to being mediocre writers or asking me what I thought of the draft's quality. Other students, however, seemed much more fluent, able to focus on what they were doing and immersing themselves into their developing ideas. Realizing that these differences could point to important aspects of the students' models of writing, I found that I needed a linguistic theory for moving beyond mere impressions and toward a recognition of distinct patterns in the students' talk.

Shuttling between theory and data, I found that Halliday's (1973) functional approach to language best captured what I was observing informally in the taped accounts. Halliday posits that language (he focuses mainly on oral communication) can be understood from three functional perspectives. The *ideational* function relates to the speaker's content—the expression of the speaker's "experience of the phenomena of the external world, and of the internal world of [his or her] own consciousness" (p. 17). The *interpersonal* function relates to the way in which the speaker participates, through language, in a social context. This function allows the speaker to take on a role in relation to others, expressing judgments, attitudes, and personality. The *textual* function refers to the actual fabric of language—its linguistic substance, the way it formally conveys the other functions through its texture.

In writing, these three language functions operate in much the same way as speech, although the context of the interaction between the writer and his or her readers may be quite different. The ideational function refers to the writer's expression of what we often call "content." The interpersonal function concerns the ways in which the writing connects with or is used to mediate among other people in a socially determined context (a classroom, a publication, a shared setting in which texts represent a kind of dialogue among participants). In more conventional compositional terms, this function typically refers to the concepts of audience and purpose. Finally, the textual function relates to the formal characteristics of the writing on a page—at the levels of theme, paragraph, sentence, and word. It is the function most often associated with the "technique" of writing—its style, structure or organization, sentence construction, lexis, use of punctuation, and the like.

As I listened and relistened to the tapes, I realized that in addition to these three useful distinctions, something more was at work in the students' talk. Some students seemed to focus on their drafts in the past tense, describing their writing processes, their decisions, the research they had done prior to writing. The texts appeared fixed, unyielding in their finality. Other students seemed to talk in the future tense, about further investigation they needed to do, about possibilities for restructuring their papers, or about what they would glean from peer readers (and from me) that they might use in a revised draft. Still other students seemed to shift back and forth between the past of the composing and the future of their revision. Sometimes these shifts would lead them to make discoveries as they talked on the tape, and they would jot down notes on the drafts or cross out words or sentences. The more tapes I studied, the more compelling became this orientation of time in the students' talk.

After some weeks of speculation, I developed a rubric for more closely analyzing the taped accounts. Along one axis, I placed Halliday's functional categories—ideational, interpersonal, textual. Along the other axis, I placed three time-oriented dimensions (past, present, and future), but translated these into terms more relevant to the evolution of the writer's text. *Retrospective* comments focus on what the writer says he or she did during the process of creating the text. *Projective* comments focus on actions (rhetorical, linguistic, informational, etc.) that the writer says he or she intends to take with the draft in order to move it forward or finish it. The final type of comment I chose to call, for lack of a better term, *temporal*; it occurs in the momentary present tense enabled by the process of recording the taped account, and includes comments in which the writer talks about the text as it is (not as it was done or as it might be changed). The sense of the text being "at rest" is no doubt a product of the surrounding curriculum; students had reached a point when they could share a full rough draft of a paper, and this point therefore took on the characteristics of an intellectual pause. However, comments of this kind often involved moments of discovery, which made them more clearly productive and analytical than purely descriptive. One interesting aspect of writers' talk at this point in the evolution of a text, therefore, is how often and in what ways static, temporal observations enable or facilitate projections for revision.

Having created a rubric for studying the taped accounts, I then began glossing transcriptions of tapes with codes representing the nine possible combinations from the rubric's two axes (functional/time-oriented):

R/ID: Retrospective/Ideational:
        "I had a strong urge to write about the issue of animal rights because I'd seen atrocities in the lab where I worked last summer."
R/IN: Retrospective/Interpersonal:
        "I was trying to convince people that no human cause justifies animal torture in lab experiments."
R/T: Retrospective/Textual:
        "I found myself using angry words in this section."

TP/ID: Temporal/Ideational:
        "The idea here also focuses on the subsidiary issue of products like shampoo that are developed as a result of animal testing."
TP/IN: Temporal/Interpersonal:
        "I can imagine someone feeling attacked by the end."
TP/T: Temporal/Textual:
        "There's a balance of long and short sentences in the middle section."

P/ID: Projective/Ideational:
        "What I hope to do is to learn more about specific cases of abuse of animals."
P/IN: Projective/Interpersonal:
        "I want to send this to some researchers who use animals and see how they react to my points."
P/T: Projective/Textual:
        "I need to switch the last and first paragraphs."

Clearly, the categories themselves are flexible. A comment like, "In this paragraph, I tried to convince the opposition that animal testing is often cruel" contains retrospective examples of all three language functions. Because they are contained in different syntactic units of the sentence, however, the sentence itself can be glossed for all three. In some cases when a single clause or an entire sentence contains more than one function or temporal perspective, it is necessary to gloss it "multiply." At first obsessed with making the categories perfectly match the texts, I eventually resolved to accept general tendencies based on careful readings, rather than statistical counts or percentages of categories for each text.

I began the analysis by selecting accounts that represented the very best and worst writers in the classes in which I used the taped method. By way of illustration, consider first the taped commentary of a particularly strong writer, Jim. A first-year student, Jim was writing a position paper on the problem of the disenchantment of the American public with the political process, as this is reflected in voter registration. He had produced a rough draft of his paper and was now creating his taped commentary:

1 **[TP/ID]:** I'm, I realize that though I stated that I'm talking about solutions for
2 low voting and low student registration in college students, **[P/ID]:** what I'm
3 really concerned about is something **[R/T]:** I said at the end of the second
4 paragraph—**[R/IN; R/ID]:** that students need to somehow know and feel the
5 impact of voting in their life. **[P/ID]:** This is really the thing that I want to
6 address my issues to and my solutions to **[P/IN]:** because there's this
7 widespread belief that our vote doesn't count in this system. **[TP/ID]:** And
8 to a certain point that is true, but it isn't always true, and **[P/ID]:** there's got to be
9 ways that recognition can be made clear. **[R/T]:** And it came true for me in
10 my example **[R/ID]:** about my district representative possibly being a
11 conservative man. This is what induced me inside to vote and to realize that
12 local elections and local campaigns and local politicians as well as federal
13 government officials have an impact on my life. **[P/IN]:** And that's
14 what I want to, I mean, how to induce that, I mean, having that change inside
15 people is what's going to call them to vote. **[P/IN]:** And I think that by
16 doing that by targeting an audience, targeting a specific group, trying to
17 inform them, is a way to induce that change inside. **[P/T; P/ID]:** I think what I
18 need to do is maybe move, change my focus a little bit, not just focusing on
19 just finding solutions for low registration, but just saying that the solution is
20 bringing up to the surface the importance to people's personal lives of voting,
21 and registering, and focusing my solutions on how to induce that. **[P/T]:** I
22 think mainly what I need to do is some reorganizing. **[P/T; P/ID]:** I'm also
23 wondering about, um, you know, I'm wondering if I say enough; do I need to
24 be saying more about the process of registration, am I needing to do more
25 informative kinds of information-giving stuff here. I might need to dig a
26 little bit. I don't know. I'll have to think about that.

A brief glance at Jim's metacommentary shows that he alternates consistently among the various functional categories, with the ideational rather more strongly represented than the textual or the interpersonal. He also shifts in time between reflecting on what he *did* and what he *needs to do*; as he reflects on the text before him and his creation of it, he also projects his process of revision—he uses phrases like "what I need to do is . . . ," "I might need to . . . ," and "this is the thing I want to address. . . ." The text is, for him, a work in progress, but that progress involves further textual decisions that he will need to make as he reconsiders his ideas and reassesses his purpose and audience. His immersions into the ideational function—even to the point of an oral embellishment of his writing—are spurred on by his uncovering what appear to be tacitly made decisions. In lines 1–3, for example, his scrutiny of "something he said at the end of the second paragraph" leads him to make an important observation about what he "really wants to say" (and presumably will spell out more carefully in his revision).

Even more interesting in Jim's commentary is the relationship between his tentativeness and his ownership of his future decisions—a relationship that, as I point out later, seems central to the difference between strong and weak writers. The tentativeness shows clearly in the shifts from retrospective or temporal comments to rather uncertain ideas for his revision. His reflection on the text before him and his creation of it uncovers tacitly made decisions that can expose new problems. These problems yield uncertainties that must (and will) be resolved in revision. Jim's acceptance of this uncertainty also shows in the way he qualifies his ideas with "maybe" or "I'm wondering" in his use of rhetorical questions directed to himself ("do I need to be saying . . . "), and in his expression of the need for more information.

In contrast to Jim's taped account, consider the one recorded by Tom. Tom is, like Terry, a struggling writer whose work to this point in the course was somewhat less than adequate:

1 Um, let's see . . . [R/T]: it went pretty smooth for me. I'll just basically tell
2 what happened; it's already done; I'm just looking at it right now, telling a bit
3 about it. [Aborted R/ID]: I, it started out with . . . [R/T]: my first paragraph
4 [R/IN]: I thought I'd catch your attention. [R/T]: As I got toward the end, I
5 started having trouble with endings and things like that. [P/IN]: So maybe
6 you could look at that and see if anything is wrong there. [R/IN]: I thought
7 maybe it was good, but I don't know. [R/T]: I had a little trouble with the
8 titles, too; I tried some of the, uh, the author [of the textbook], whatever his
9 name was again, can't remember it offhand, but like I tried some of his tactics,
10 wrote down a lot of titles, some I liked, you know, a lot I didn't like too, but
11 still couldn't come up with one. And that's about it. This is Tom, signing off.

Although, like Jim, Tom shifts around a bit among functions, his talk is still dominated by the textual function described retrospectively. The text's substance—everything between the first paragraph and the troubled ending—is ignored. In fact, Tom offers little commentary about his ideas, and only a vague reference to the dynamics of audience (grabbing the reader's attention). In short, Tom's discussion seems almost atrophied intellectually, as if now that the words are on paper, there is little more to say about them until some teacherly judgment comes his way.

Also contrasting with Jim's account is Tom's deference to my authority as the teacher. This appears in a redundant opener possibly designed to apprise me that he has, in fact, completed the paper. It also appears in the second-person address ("I thought I'd catch your attention"; "maybe you could look at that"). Bound by impending judgment, Tom seems unable to move his writing forward or even say much about it. Whereas Jim's uncertainty appears productive, Tom seems embarrassed by his, as if at once disclosing weakness, expecting help, and asking obliquely for praise ("maybe you'll think it's good"). Interestingly, some proficient writers also seemed aware of me as a "listener," but appeared to make the tapes a more integral part of their projects. The tapes were a chance for outsiders, even a teacher, to look over their shoulders as they crafted their papers. These abler students were not the least embarrassed by the uncertainties expressed in their in-process, tentative comments; on the contrary, they seemed to embrace uncertainty as a natural part of their writing, using it to weigh alternatives as they used the moment of intellectual pause for some reflection.

TOWARD AN UNDERSTANDING OF STUDENTS' MODELS OF WRITING

The metacommentaries of strong writers suggest productive models of the writing process, models of writers "in control" of their own texts, even when they may lack certain strategies for success. In contrast, the metacommentaries of weak writers frequently defer to authority, giving up ownership (if it were ever there) for the sake of submission to law and norms to which they do not have access. Such students fear uncertainty, perhaps attributing it to ignorance or inability—precisely the opposite of what appears to drive stronger writers. Frequently, the weak writers' statements of uncertainty and deference to authority also accompanied language suggesting a highly dualistic approach to writing. Texts are either "correct" or "incorrect," "right" or "wrong" (recall Terry's reference in line 6 to something being "wrong" in his text). The following excerpt is typical:

> I think I wrote a pretty balanced paper except I'm not sure if it's organized *the right way with the right paragraphs*. I don't think . . . the paragraphs might not be in, *where they should be*. [italics added]

In the next two excerpts, we see writers linking the sense of a "right way" with guesses about the teacher's expectations for a paper:

> Um, I went to the library and got some good stuff. And I interviewed my hometown—well, he owns a liquor store, and I know his, I knew him kind of, well, not *too* well, you know, I knew of him, and he knew me by name, I guess, but I was kind of pressed for time and stuff, so I just did him. Probably a little more easy than what . . . *you probably wanted me to interview somebody a little bit harder.* [italics added]

> Hi. Let me tell you that I realize my paper's a little bit long; um, I have a tendency to babble on about different parts in my paper. . . . *I don't know if this is what you wanted* in the paper, you know, it's supposed to be about a significant event . . . . [italics added]

As suggested here, students who lack control of their own writing seldom comment projectively, because there is little room for their own decision-making process in revision. Instead, they measure their texts against what must be a very sketchy, nebulous image of the teacher's "standards," an image they try to fill in and clarify from various sources (including direct appeal). Ironically, the tapes themselves, designed to create an opportunity for reflection, become for these students an extension of the process of teacherly judgment.

In his work extending the scheme of intellectual development first presented by William Perry, Newman (1993) has proposed three somewhat less lockstep stages through which young adults pass in their attitudes toward knowledge. *Absolutism* is characterized by a belief in the absolute truth or falsity of knowledge. "Because facts about the world can be fully determined, strong absolutists reject personal responsibility for ideas and decisions" (Charney, Newman, & Palmquist, 1995, p. 302). *Relativism* refers to the learner's denial that truth can be determined—knowledge is just subjective opinion, so anything goes. *Evaluatism*, however, accepts various opinions and beliefs, but does so from a conviction that some ideas are more valid (better reasoned, more logical, etc.) than others. An evaluatist might entertain four different and contradictory suggestions for the revision of a problematic paragraph, but finally reject three of them based on a careful assessment of their improvement (or lack thereof).

In considering the metacommentaries of students who take or lack "control" of their texts, not surprisingly these distinctions bear fruit. There is an unmistakably "absolutist" quality in the metacommentaries of students who speak of their writing textually and in the past tense, and there is an unmistakably "evaluatistic" quality in the talk of both successful novice writers and experienced writers as they shift among functions, retrospect and project, and embrace uncertainty in their own control of their work.

Also reflected in these tendencies may be the relationship between students' attitudes toward learning and their perceptions of their own writing processes and abilities to succeed. Reviewing the literature associated with beliefs about learning and their connection to scholastic achievement, Charney et al. (1995) have noted:

> Active learners are more likely to see intelligence as a mutable quality that they can refine with attention and practice. Active learners are challenged by difficult tasks; if they fail, they try again or consider other strategies for succeeding the next time. Their primary goal is to *develop* their competencies rather than to *judge* their competence. Less active learners tend to see intelligence as a fixed, one-time, lump-sum allotment that either is or is not sufficient for the task at hand. . . . The profile of passive learners suggests that viewing writing ability as a lump-sum allotment or gift may discourage students from investing much effort in learning to write. (p. 300)

Finally, although students seemed to cluster into those who, on the one hand, showed movement among the categories in the rubric and those who, on the other, immersed themselves in the retrospective/textual function, it is worth noting that not all students fell neatly into what may by now appear to be two distinct models of writing. Most common in this group were those who became immersed in the ideational function, either retrospectively or temporally, and never shifted to issues of text, purpose, or audience. In this tape, for example, a student is writing about watching the twin foals of a mare die at birth:

1 [R/ID]: The more and more that I think about it, there's more and more
2 experiences that happened to me. And just one that seems to stick out in my
3 mind is when a brood mare that we had at our hobby farm delivered twins.
4 And I guess I never had been really close to a lot of death or watching
5 something really die, other than, you know, we've had dogs and cats die, and,
6 um, and another premature foal die. But this one, it seemed to affect me so

7 much more than anything had ever affected me before. I was just astounded,
8 and, uh, it's made me think a lot about life, and living, and how fortunate we
9 humans are, with all the technology we have, to keep so many different
10 things alive, it's just a miracle. You know, people gripe about how so many
11 people die from so many different diseases. [continues in R/ID for 9 minutes]
12 It was so, oh, I can't even describe the feeling it was to be there with those
13 animals. And they knew what was going on; they weren't themselves, you
14 know . . . . [continues in R/ID for 6 minutes]

Like students whose talk was dominated by retrospective/textual commentary, most students caught in the ideational function were also typically weaker writers. Although no informal analysis like this one can yield foolproof conclusions or razor-sharp patterns, it appears that there is a strong relationship between proficiency and the blending/shifting of functions in scheme I had developed. The strongest writers, in other words, moved freely between functions and the time-related stages of text production.

TEACHING OF MODELS: THE INFLUENCE ON PRACTICE

In this description of several informal, classroom-based studies, I have tried to suggest some ways in which educators can read students' reflective commentaries on their work, using one set of perspectives informed by theory and repeated observation. Like any raw material from students, their metacommentaries may be read for many other useful, and unique, perspectives. I did not, for example, deliberately set out to analyze the taped accounts through the lenses of gender differences, cultural influences, aspects of students' personalities, or correlations to other measures of intellectual ability. Yet, although my scope was limited to patterns I could easily discern without a large or complicated analytical apparatus, I was nevertheless surprised by the consistency with which struggling writers fell into the model of "teacher in control," as reflected in their commentaries.

In my subsequent practice, I have tried to draw on this observation in helping young writers to think about their work in less stifling and more productive ways. By designing open-ended assignments that offer the safety of instructional support while they also challenge students to make their own decisions, I try to help students to own their writing and see it in a less static, performance-based way. By creating opportunities for multiple readings of students' writing, especially through peer groups, I have tried to show students the importance of feedback in helping to use indeterminacy to their advantage. By asking students to tell me more about their own intentions, I can prompt them to go beyond a mere report of "having done something" and toward a discussion of their struggles and possible directions. Finally, by responding to their writing in questioning, student-centered ways, I can continue to redirect their authorial decisions back on to them, compelling them to make hard choices or experiment with possibilities until they reach resolution (see Straub & Lunsford, 1995).

In listening to students talk about writing, I have come to value the development of their models of writing even more than I value the improvement in their texts. If we limit ourselves instructionally only to the refinement of individual products, some students may succeed at the tasks we set them without growing in their relationship with their work. Students will always write texts of comparatively uneven quality, some much better than others; this is a characteristic of all writers. However, once they begin thinking about writing productively, they stand a much better chance of developing expertise and working more successfully in future writing situations.

REFERENCES

Berkenkotter, C. (1983). Decisions and revisions: The planning strategies of a publishing writer. *College Composition and Communication*, 34(2), 156-169.

Carter, K. (1993). The place of story in the study of teaching and teacher education. *Educational Researcher*, 22, 5-12.

Charney, D., Newman, J. H., & Palmquist, M. (1995). "I'm just no good at writing": Epistemological style and attitudes toward writing. *Written Communication*, 12, 298-329.

Emig, J. (1971). *The composing processes of twelfth graders*. Urbana, IL: National Council of Teachers of English.

Ericsson, K. A., & Simon, H. A. (1980). Verbal reports as data. *Psychological Review*, 87(3), 215-251.

Ericsson, K. A., & Simon, H. A. (1984). *Protocol analysis: Verbal reports as data*. Cambridge, MA: MIT Press.

Finley, T. B. (1995). *Post-baccalaureate pre-service English teachers' narratives, stances, roles and practice*. Unpublished doctoral dissertation, University of Minnesota.

Flower, L., & Hayes, J. (1977). Problem-solving strategies and the writing process. *College English*, 39, 449-461.

Flower, L., & Hayes, J. (1980). The dynamics of composing: Making plans and juggling constraints. In L. Gregg & E. Steinberg (Eds.),

Cognitive processes in writing: An interdisciplinary approach (pp. 31–50). Hillsdale, NJ: Erlbaum.

Flower, L., & Hayes, J. (1981). Plans that guide the composing process. In C. H. Frederickson & J. F. Dominic (Eds.), *Writing: The nature, development, and teaching of written communication* (pp. 39-58). Hillsdale, NJ: Erlbaum.

Halliday, M. A. K. (1973). *Explorations in the functions of language.* London: Edward Arnold.

Newman, J. H. (1993). A structural investigation of intellectual development and epistemological style in young adults. *Dissertation Abstracts International, 54,* 2786B.

Odell, L., Goswami, D., & Herrington, A. (1983). The discourse-based interview: A procedure for exploring the tacit knowledge of writers in non-academic settings. In P. Mosenthal, L. Tamor, & S. A. Walmsley (Eds.), *Research on writing: Principles and methods* (pp. 221–236). New York: Longman.

Odell, L., Goswami, D., & Quick, D. (1983). Writing outside the English composition class: Implications for teaching and learning. In R. W. Bailey & R. M. Fosheim (Eds.), *Literacy for life: The demand for reading and writing* (pp. 175–194). New York: MLA.

Polanyi, M. (1966). *The tacit dimension.* Garden City, NY: Doubleday.

Rose, M. (1980). Rigid rules, inflexible plans, and the stifling of language: A cognitivist analysis of writer's block. *College Composition and Communication, 31,* 389-400.

Smagorinsky, P. (1989). The reliability and validity of protocol analysis. *Written Communication, 6,* 463-479.

Steinberg, E. (1986). Protocols, retrospective reports, and the stream of consciousness. *College English, 48(7),* 697-704.

Straub, R., & Lunsford, R. (1995). *Twelve readers reading.* Cresskill, NJ: Hampton Press.

Tomlinson, B. (1984). Talking about the composing process: The limitations of retrospective accounts. *Written Communication, 1,* 429-445.

5 CONFESSIONS FROM OUR REFLECTIVE CLASSROOM*

Sam Watson

University of North Carolina-Charlotte

> Thought is confession, drawing out notions that do not dare show themselves.
> —*Student in an expository writing class*

Should we put our trust in "self-assessment"? Personally I am reluctant to, for several reasons. "Assessment" seems a short step—although possibly a positive one—from "evaluation." Evaluation is a necessary part of education (and of life), but in my experience it is easy for the evaluative tail to begin wagging the educational dog. When that happens, even if the evaluators are working from the best of motives, we and our students soon suffer reductive consequences. What is more, I am not sure what "self-assessment" might come to mean. Although no one intends it, the very language of the phrase invites one's assessment, not of writing being done, but of his or her self. Also, I am not at all sure what might be the sources for standards of such assessment. Even granting the good intentions that what one is being asked to assess is her or his writing and writing development, our culture still exhibits an Enlightenment bias within which standards are external or objective. I do not share that

---

*The "I" of this chapter is Sam Watson, who takes full responsibility for what is said here. However, in the writing of it, Ms. Rashida Ahsan, then a graduate student at UNC Charlotte, served as participant/observer in the writing class that provided the most immediate crucible for these reflections. In all ways other than the actual drafting of (and responsibility for) these words, Ms. Ahsan is a co-author of this chapter.

orientation. From my perspective, informed by my understanding of Michael Polanyi, for one to impose externally set standards would more likely lead to alienation from one's own writing and perhaps from one's own self, rather than to the development of either.

Many of my students seem already to have been evaluated or assessed to death; their lifeless presence in my classes does not give me much hope for evaluation or even assessment as a route for deepening the quality of their education or their lives. Although I harbor these doubts about self-assessment, I do believe in self-reflection. When my students come to me, however, I do not often see that self-reflection is playing any significant role in their lives. The most important goal in my writing classes—more important, I think, even than the production of polished writing—is to help students change that.

I understand self-reflection quite simply: It is thinking about what you are doing while you are doing it, and the thinking is often called forth by something problematic in the doing. That is quite different from thinking instead of doing, which could be a shorthand definition of procrastination. It is also quite different from doing without thinking. That attitude, which presumes that any necessary "thinking" has already been done, probably by somebody else and certainly independent of the context of the doing, may have become typical practice throughout our culture and in our students' work. I see it, for example, in the nearly universal reports from my students, that teachers' specification of some form for their writing serves, contrary to teachers' good intentions, to replace the students' own thinking rather than to extend or deepen their thinking. I cannot ask students to engage in reflection unless I do so myself. Hence this chapter, which I intend as an instance of self-reflection.

Aside perhaps from the tautologies of mathematical proofs, no meaningful text stands alone, including this one. Behind it lies my reading, largely a layman's reading, of Schön (1983, 1987, 1991) and other proponents of "reflective practice." In effect, I am trying to help my students become reflective practitioners, with respect to their writing, yes, but I hope also with respect to their living. Writing can serve as a powerful means to the end of reflective practice, and writing seems most powerfully developed when the writing serves as means to something beyond itself. Therefore, although my orientation is not the best one for all students, I do not think that I am neglecting the development of my students' writing.

Also informing this reflection and lying more immediately behind it, is my understanding of Michael Polanyi. Both the subject and a reader of my dissertation (Watson, 1973), Polanyi has been my most abiding intellectual mentor ever since. This confession thus consists of some introduction to Polanyi, via my reading of him; my understanding of what writing is and does, expressed largely in a family of metaphors that often become a sort of lingua franca in my classes; a sense of what typically happens in one of my classes; finally, the outcomes my students express via their writing—most especially their sense of change in their attitudes toward their writing and toward themselves—and my readings of what they are saying.

Perhaps it is already obvious, but I want my class—actually, it is *our* class, as I ask my students to say and believe—to be a dialogic one, in much the sense that Stock (1995) developed. I try very hard to listen to students, to take seriously what they say, to learn from and with them. The listening may indeed be the most important thing that I do, for both myself and my students. Thus quotes from students will show up, in italics, throughout these pages. *This is the only class I have where the professor takes notes when the students talk.*

How does reflection work? How do we go about doing it, and why? In Schön's (1987) terms, some problems are ones of "technical rationality." These are resolved by working data through preexisting formulae or formulations. Other problems, however, remain problematic in the face of such manipulations. Reflection is called for when a problem for whatever reason resists our existing formulation of it, when it turns out not quite to fit the existing categories of our understanding. It is hardly too much to suggest that we engage in reflection when we find that we are "without arts or systems to guide us," as Aristotle (1941) long ago said when he located rhetorical invention with respect to the other arts.

Under Enlightenment influences, rhetorical invention gave way to the presumed certainties of scientific method. However, scientific method, it turns out, is not nearly so certain as it has seemed in recent centuries, and the identification of "science" with "certainty" has had unfortunate consequences for our culture at large and for the work of science itself. In science, for instance, it has called attention to matters of verification, increasingly leaving out of the picture altogether any attention to matters of discovery.

MY REFLECTIVE READING OF MICHAEL POLANYI

The process of examining any topic is both an exploration of the topic, and an exegesis of our fundamental beliefs in light of which we approach it; a dialectical combination of exploration and exegesis. Our fundamental beliefs are continually reconsidered in the course of such a process, but only within the scope of their own basic premises.
—Michael Polanyi, 1964a, p. 267

Michael Polanyi's central philosophic mission was to trace the dynamics of discovery, finding within scientific activity itself broad and important implications for our understanding of human endeavors generally. In so doing, he cleared philosophic space for actions of reflection; "discovery," indeed, could be seen as "reflection" writ large.

Polanyi's (1964a) central philosophic text is titled *Personal Knowledge*,[1] and his abiding claim is that all knowledge is either personal or is rooted in personal knowledge—*all* knowledge. Polanyi was not some bleary-eyed romantic. His philosophy is not an invitation to self-indulgence but to inquiry. As first a research scientist himself, Polanyi (1969) saw that the most abiding and the most foundational dimension of science is active inquiry in quest of discovery, and inquiry is something that persons undertake. Within our human worlds we inquire naturally, by virtue of being persons and by use of the language we inhabit. "A truly human intellect dwells in us only when our lips shape words and our eyes read print" (p. 160).

If science is seen as rigorously impersonal, there turns out to be no place for scientific work itself. However, we have come to view the world increasingly through just such a distorting lens, with consequences far beyond the realms of science. Such a vision has no place for persons as centers of consciousness worthy of being understood and deserving of respect.

We can know more than we can tell. Beneath our telling as beneath our knowing lies our tacit embodiment of all on which we depend and through which we explore all that is beyond ourselves. Our explorations oblige us to rely on matters we could never exhaustively specify or demonstrably prove, and our reliance includes our trust in ourselves and in one another as agents of knowing, generally reliable though never infallible.

My use of a simple probe to establish contact with something beyond myself, that I cannot touch directly, illustrates the dynamics of Polanyi's "tacit knowing." At first I handle the probe clumsily, aware of little more than its awkward, unfamiliar feel in my hand. Soon, however, the feel of the probe against my hand becomes subsidiary; my

---

[1]Although *Personal Knowledge* is Polanyi's (1964a) central philosophic work, his other books are shorter and may be more accessible. For reliable, book-length introductions to his thought, see Gelwick (1977), Scott (1985), and Prosch (1986). Poteat (1985, 1990, 1994) gave us especially searching implications and extensions of Polanyi's thought. Those interested can join scholars from a number of disciplines in The Polanyi Society (Richard Gelwick, University of New England, Biddeford, ME 04005; ph. 207/283-0171). Polanyi's thought has received considerable attention from scholars of rhetoric and composition. See Booth (1974); Elbow, Emig, Phelps, Wallace, and Watson (1990-91); and Watson (1973, 1981a, 1981b, 1981c).

consciousness shifts outward, as the probe becomes an extension of myself and I attend to what its other end is touching. A similar process happens with visual perception: As the Gestaltist psychologists have shown, a coherent view is something I construct, from constellations of cues. Sensory data that were initially confusing I somehow resolve into "ground" and "figure," with "ground" being, like the movements and tensions of my eyes themselves, subsidiary to the "figure" to which my attention has become directed. I come to make out the focal figure through an act of tacit integration, not through formal inference. In even the act of visual perception, I commit myself to tacit standards that I necessarily set for myself. "Perception is manifestly an activity which seeks to satisfy standards which it sets to itself" (Polanyi, 1964a, p. 96).

Whether the field of inquiry is perceptual or conceptual, the moment of insight is likely to be sudden, largely irreversible, and possibly mistaken. Having solved a visual puzzle, I can hardly unsolve it; I am no longer able to see it as a puzzle even though, as optical illusions illustrate, my solution might be mistaken. Likewise a conceptual discovery; my initial commitment to its possible truth focuses my interest and invests my energies in its further exploration. Even if I am a scientist working within a well-established disciplinary framework, there can be no formal criteria which guarantee success. Necessarily, "[The scientist] is himself the ultimate judge of what he accepts as true" (Polanyi, 1964b, p. 38). That is not to say that the scientist works by whim: "In a competent mental act the agent does not do as he pleases, but compels himself forcibly to act as he believes he must. He can do no more, and he would evade his calling by doing less" (1964a, p. 315). Although committed to the truth of a discovery being achieved, even the scientist could quite possibly be mistaken.

For these reasons, inherently persuasive acts are essential to inquiry and to acceptance of its findings. Polanyi (1964a) wrote:

> Proponents of a new system can convince their audience only by winning their intellectual sympathy for a doctrine they have not yet grasped. . . . [Proponents must teach the others] a new language, and no one can learn a new language unless he first trusts that it means something. . . . Those who listen sympathetically will discover for themselves what they would otherwise never have understood. Such an acceptance is a heuristic process, a self-modifying act, and to this extent a conversion. (p. 151)

When we are engaged in inquiry, the terms of our language act not so much like containers of predefined meanings; they act instead like probes, whose meanings we may find changed within our achievement of insight. Words act, in a word, metaphorically, and metaphors act heuristically. "I believe that in spite of the hazards involved, I am called upon to search for the truth and state my findings" (1964a, p. 299). In that deceptively simple sentence, Polanyi summarized his own philosophic orientation. It is an orientation within which the self-awareness we call "reflection" finds a natural home.

METAPHORIC UNDERSTANDINGS OF WRITING

> When we discover that we have in this world no earth or rock to stand or walk upon but only shifting sea and sky and wind, the mature response is not to lament the loss of fixity but to learn to sail.
> —James Boyd White, 1984, p. 278

Why and how do we actually go about writing? What terms might enable us to respond most richly to such a query? The first question invites reflection; the second calls for a medium in which we might reflect. Reflection does require a medium, whose generic name is "language." In our class, questions such as these provide a perpetual undercurrent, encouraging us to reflect on the writing in which we are engaged. We find ourselves developing a language for what we are doing, and that language seems to be inherently metaphorical. The metaphors that follow are not "right" (indeed one wondrous property of metaphors is that they all are by definition "wrong" in some sense!), but these are clusters of metaphor that have developed with some consistency over the years in our reflective classroom. *The little metaphors that you mention in class, [which] I write down in my notebook, and then later see again, are what really help me the most.* I invite students to develop their own terms, but I also invite them to watch the ways in which they begin as metaphors or turn metaphorical as they look through the lenses their terms provide.

Metaphors seem to encourage new insights or to reawaken us more deeply to what we already know. They have the convenient property of being literally false. Thus it is difficult to hear a metaphoric language with literalistic ears. Rather than hearing rules to be mindlessly applied as dicta, we find ourselves invited to get inside the metaphors instead, to see the world of our own writing from the perspectives those metaphors offer. *On metaphors where you ask students to "imagine something they have not yet grasped," I feel it is not only that; but also, each student has their own idea or interpretation of the metaphor. Therefore the various experiences of each individual create different effects on different students.*

Metaphors become our medium of reflection on writing. *Through the use of a metaphor, we as students and writers can interpret as we see fit. Each interpretation is separate and original.* Valuable in its own right, our metaphoric turn also helps prepare students for the times when their own writing will turn "metaphoric," often much to their own surprise and sometimes dismay. T.S. Eliot (1962) complained, "Words strain,/ Crack and sometimes break, under the burden,/ Under the tension, slip, slide, perish,/ Decay with imprecision, will not stay in place,/ Will not stay still" (p. 121). He is registering the sort of disequilibrium any writer experiences whose words have come to serve not merely as inert containers of predetermined meanings, but as probes and clues to something beyond the words themselves, to new insights. In the service of unexpected coherences, the sense of words often shifts, and reflective writers need to become comfortable with such shifts. In White's (1984) terms, our task is to learn to sail. *I feel that my writing has a mind of its own. It seems to throw itself on the paper and organize itself in its own way. I feel that my writing has also found itself going into a direction that is never-ending. I can explore my thoughts on anything I like. I don't have to stick to one certain topic. I can go all over. / I've spent so much time—valuable time—in the past, tearing up my papers and starting over constantly, that it was beginning to get ridiculous. It was taking me forever to produce even the shortest piece. For the last two papers I've turned in to you I've tried something different. I started beginning each paper with even the most awkward statement and stuck with it—reworking and reshaping things, trying desperately not to let myself get pissed and toss it. It was a difficult thing to do, and took a long time to do it. The whole thing turned into my own personal project. But in the end I was rather proud of myself. You know what? I'm a writer!*

"Fish swim in water; we humans swim in language." That metaphor is remarkable only for its understatement. Language is the medium, usually transparent, within which we move. *We have been learning how to view language as a medium in which we exist, rather than simply a device we use.* The metaphor should stir the medium some, making it just a bit murky, rendering it somewhat visible. *I [now look] at writing as a "being" in itself, rather than just a transparent mode of explaining something.* Students should begin sensing the ways that languages are giving shape and direction to the worlds in which they live. *Language has become much more than a means of communication. It is a reflection of who we are and where we are in society. Language shapes us just as much as we shape it. That had never occurred to me before and now it seems so disgustingly obvious.* Students should also discover their own language, orally and in writing, to be an extension of themselves and a shaper of their own worlds, rather than something alien to them. *I found that writing is a method I can use to find what I didn't know that lies under the surface of my mind. I never really knew that writing could help me in this way.*

"Writing floats in a sea of talk." Who of us would write at all, if the writing did not takes its impetus and its bearings from the inherently informal and essentially unbounded talk in which others and we engage? Who would write, except somehow to contribute to that conversation? *If I could only write down exactly what I had said in the conversation with my friend! You have shown us that writing is this conversation with a friend, only now the friend may be the paper. . . . If we learn to interact with the topic instead of trying to tame it, our writing will improve. The same seems to be true of reading.*

Conversation is seldom clear; neither is composing. Throughout their educational lives, well-intentioned demands for clarity seem especially to have frustrated my students' writing development. "Clarity" seems to imply that texts "contain" meaning, but they do not. I think I can see my students struggling for words large enough to "contain" the meanings they would like to express, a dynamic that helps account for the overly abstract character of much student writing. Because we can know more than we can tell, any serious attempt to have a text "tell all" is a movement toward tautology, purchasing clarity at the price of emptiness. *I started off the semester viewing my writing as somewhat of a transparent mode of explaining things. [But] I began to realize that writing is an active process that isn't complete without true involvement from the writer. Then I realized that what was missing from MY writing wasn't description, but thought. I wasn't placing MYSELF into my writing. As soon as I became more involved with what I was writing, many of the pressures that I used to feel began to lift.*

Composing is much more like the weaving of cloth; indeed, "text" is instructively cognate with "texture" and "textile" (Miller, 1986). And one never weaves cloth, if all the threads run in the same direction. Without tensions between its threads, cloth would not hold together. "Focus" is never on some one thing (it's not a matter of "narrowing your subject") but a felt convergence of differences, of "(increasingly) focused *tensions." I realize that I can say what I need to say, and it will be clear to my reader, too, if I concentrate less on the form and more on the focus.* In what I am sure is egregious etymology, I invite students to think of "attention" as "at-tension," placing oneself *between* some things, and of "interest" similarly as "inter-est," as placing ourselves *between* some things which jointly draw us forward. And I invite us to think of texts, depending on their purpose and genre, as either inviting us to create such tensions within ourselves or as responding to the tensions which we bring to the texts. *What can I do to catch the attention of others and have them hang on the edge of their seats as they read? My attitude toward writing has changed, and I believe that was 90% of my problem in the past. One thing that I have discovered through my writing this semester is that the excitement that was missing before, is there now.*

Oysters make pearls; humans make language, for something of the same reasons. If some grain of sand had not become an irritant to us, we would scarcely do it. *An oyster lives and dies in a hard shell. Likewise so does our writing when we learn to write for and like others. What is produced may be good to the taste but it is soon gone, leaving only indigestion. In this hard mold, our writing will produce something but maybe not a part of ourselves. Conversely a pearl is made from a grain of sand. At first this grain is an irritant. So also is writing when you first start to explore while still in the mold. Eventually, however, the grain of sand is made into a beautiful pearl which lasts a lifetime. Our writing can also be imperishable if we let it be a part of ourselves. / I write to relieve myself of frustrations, to work out my difficulties on paper. I somehow attempt to use my writing as a conversation partner, to bounce ideas on paper and see what returns to me, in the form of possible solutions or, at the least, a better understanding of what my problem is.*

Some activities enervate us, sapping us of energy; engaged in others, we produce new energies. So it is with writing (and with reading). I don't want to supervise the sapping of strength, but rather to foster our production of new energies. *At times it was tedious and most certainly frustrating. Yet, I have never felt the depth of passion, a movement of what must be sacred energy within me, that I have only begun to experience in writing.* Writing is a matter of bringing different things together; much like the polarized but invisible energies of electrical charges, these differences can spark new energies—and new insights. *It is really weird because I would sit down with my pen and paper and have no idea what to write, when suddenly thoughts would come flying through my head. One by one I captured those flying particles and pasted them onto my paper in the form of sentences which built into stacks of ideas./ In order to paint a clear picture of our thoughts, we must be generous with our words. / When I'm putting thoughts on paper and thinking/writing things through, I can watch how ideas spark, and how these sparks spark new sparks. My writing is improving. I enjoy my writing. And it is your fault.*

Seeking the shapes within those sparks—that can be much like shining a flashlight on a worn metal mirror. The scratches organize themselves, and they do so differently as the light is shifted from one part of the mirror to another. Perhaps it is even more like placing a magnet within a scattering of iron filings: The filings organize themselves by opposition, the opposition of the magnet's polarity. Discovering such polarities is part of writing, often a matter of jotting down details, hunches, fragments of thought and asking then what "center(s) of gravity" (Elbow, 1973, p. 35) want to organize them, "centers" which *are* "centers" because, as with a balance scale, they are weights opposed to one another.

If energy is to be productively used, it must somehow be transferred to something beyond its own source. The engine of a car on blocks may hum beautifully, but the car won't go anywhere unless its tires establish traction with the road. Establishing traction with what is beyond itself—that is something which writing also must do, if it is to move anybody anywhere.

Within our class, "specific details" become less a matter of "supports" to existing ideas, and more a matter of points of traction with what is beyond the text and at the same time clues to possible qualifications or further ideas, "constellations" pointing toward something(s) as yet unknown.

"Form" is never a matter of mechanically applied "form-ula" but of change: Within the writing or because of it, some person is being invited to change her or himself from some particular state to (or toward) some other one. In writing that is personally meaningful, the change affects the writer. *I feel like we are really learning how to write with our minds, not by standard forms where you use information to fill in blanks.* "Write so that *you* remain part of your own audience" is advice I give; it's useful advice to novice writers, and I think it is ethically important advice to *any* of us. *Form is not a mechanical thing we do on the paper. Form, on the other hand, is what we do while writing. I find this a very important bit of advice.*

Where discovery and change are possibilities, tidy conclusions may not be. I invite students to think of the endings of many papers as a ski jump—a long glide down, picking up tremendous energies, then an upward curve, where the paper ends by propelling reader and writer farther than the explicit words can go.

I wish it went without saying, but I try to get students to understand that all writing is *personal* writing, in the senses I am bringing from Polanyi. Although it would be inappropriate and counterproductive for some writing to call attention *to* the personal, "the personal"—the hunches, the unexpressed and the inexpressible thoughts, the sense of some real "I" "standing behind" the words on the page—is always there, if the writing has any promise of significance. Those "personal" dimensions are a bit like the silent waters running beneath the Okeefenokee swamp, south Georgia's "land of the trembling earth," a giant peat bog that from a distance *looks* as substantial as dry land, but is sustained by the waters beneath it. *It is refreshing and encouraging to see how my personal writing stimulates me to deeper thinking and learning. When I was confused or didn't fully understand a certain point of a lecture, I would write about my questions and uncertainties regarding that topic. Most of the time, my thinking processes would enable me to comprehend the subject matter that I previously had not understood.*

When it comes to the "academic" (and apparently impersonal) papers students are being expected to write in other courses, I use a different metaphor—one of icebergs. If an iceberg is real, most of it does not show itself above the ocean's surface. If an academic paper is real, much of the "personal" likely lies beneath the surface of the page. Without the personal, one can only construct a styrofoam iceberg. As the semester goes on, incredulous students sometimes report that the grades they are receiving on those "academic" papers are actually going *up*. I *have applied what I have learned (although I was hesitant at first) to my other courses. I was pleasantly surprised to find the results were great. At last, I do not have to feel restricted by an assignment. In fact, in some of my more tedious courses, a writing assignment is not a chore, but a challenge.*

Many of our metaphors are ones of orientation, of location. This should hardly be surprising, if we remember that "topic" shares roots with "topography" and that the ancient inventional schemes were seen as "places." In effect, I am hoping that our metaphors help students see differently with respect to their own writing, enabling them to see it as something which *is* their own but not thereby completely transparent. Rather, it is translucent, something that they can continue to develop long after our course is over.

Responding to an earlier draft of this chapter, a former student wrote me: *Literally, your metaphors said NOTHING to me on the initial readings. . . . Only after I had written about my own did yours begin to MEAN. . . . This looping back and forth between your essay and my own writing now seems related to what you said about "attention." I started out with a "tension" between what I wanted to hear and what I "heard" you saying. By saying what I wanted to hear, I began to hear it in your essay. Was it there all along? Is it what you called "INTER-est"??*

Yes.

CLASS PRACTICES TO INVITE REFLECTION

Mental reflection is so much more interesting than TV it's a shame more people don't switch over to it. They probably think what they hear is unimportant but it never is.
—Robert Pirsig, 1975, p. 199

Our class wants to be a culture where writing is a medium for our living and learning, but also a subject for our continued discussing. Course policies and class time are structured to help us achieve that double stance, of simultaneous immersion in our own writing and reflection on it.

We begin with writing. Our first class session finds me reading aloud an open letter I have just written to students whom I have not yet met. In that letter I say something about myself, my background, my frustrations and satisfactions with writing, my current projects, interests (some of which seem decidedly nonacademic) and inquiries, including what *I* hope to learn in the course we are beginning together. The letter introduces me as a person learning, and doing this writing quite frankly enables me to become such a person in our class. I ask my students to respond in kind, and I then respond to each of them with an individual letter. We have begun.

Part of what we have begun is a conversation about our writing that will continue through the semester, both orally and in writing. Our first letter exchange initiates a semester-length correspondence I carry on with each student. Virtually every writing assignment comes in two parts: the requested text and a letter to me accompanying that text. In the letter, I ask students to tell me whatever they can, as much as they can, about their writing of that particular text: How did they go about doing it? What are they trying to accomplish in it? What surprises did the writing bring? What difficulties did they discover? What hunches, about the writing or the subject, have not found their way into the text itself? I do not ask that students' responses be explicitly metaphorical, but when I find that they are I rejoice, and I respond by extending or qualifying or otherwise encouraging further metaphoric thought.

In my letter responses which are usually replete with typos and misspellings (there is not time for corrections, and I want students to see that imperfect writing has its important places), I reflect on whatever the student has said and pose further questions that engage me and to which I think that student might be receptive. *I have found a unique trend in your letters. You attack the page in a jumbled syntax of confused questions, and then when you reach a point of highest perplexity, you succinctly write your way out of the morass and leave the reader somehow enlightened, but never sure how.* Writing these letters deepens my own inquiries, and it usually renders pleasurable what, without the students' letters, would often remain an onerous chore. My letters illustrate the inquiry and reflection in which I am inviting students to engage, and one of my greatest satisfactions is to see students beginning to accept that invitation. *The letters and responses gave insight to my writing capabilities where I thought I had lost them. I never really lost them, they were just too damn afraid to come out. The responses also gave insight to me from you because you let me know how you felt about my writing and how I could better it. No other teacher has ever done that. They could care less about what you think and how you feel about a paper because they feel that you're only doing it for a grade. That hurts.*

But of course the really important letters are the ones that students write. The requirement of an accompanying letter encourages them to develop a more accurate and more healthy understanding of writing's functions and its frustrations. *Oh, my God! These letters [I wrote] were lifesavers. I would get so frustrated with my papers sometimes and the only person I wanted to tell was YOU! While writing my papers I would always jot down little notes titled, What to tell Sam. This worked for me because I felt like you were listening and most of all you were concerned. I really felt so through your responses. I never turned in an assignment without letting you know how I felt. And I told myself, Very good job!* Perhaps the best payoff of all is that the writing of these letters also has a way of feeding into students' other writing. (For a more complete discussion of our use of letters, see Watson, 1990.)

Our second assignment, which came originally from the Alaska Writing Project, is almost always a sketch of a classmate to be read before the entire class. We each compose questions, as many as there are class members, on 3" x 5" cards. Each question must be one to which any member of the class could respond, and the response might say something interesting about that person. During class we shuffle the cards and jot a classmate's name on each then don name tags and conduct mini-interviews, posing the question aloud, allowing time for a thoughtful response, listening, and jotting a representation of that response on the card. We each leave that class with a stack of responses, from a person we have just begun to know, and with the assignment to read those responses, take note of what happens *while* we read them, and prepare questions for a more in-depth interview during the next class session. Then each of us composes a sketch of our subject. The sketch can be in any form, can make any use of the responses given, and its subject will have the right to silently read, correct, and make deletions before its writer reads it aloud to the class.

Hearing one's sketch read aloud and reading one's sketch of another writer authorizes each class member. We have each heard our own writing voice in public, and we have begun to know something about one another. The images are characteristically positive, and students frequently express surprise that we are such *interesting* people. As indeed we are; the fact is, the writing helps us in some measure become, for the purposes of our class, the interesting persons we have described.

Of all the writing we will do through the semester, the sketches are in some respects the most difficult. They are shaped within the constraints of "real-world" writing: limited time, incomplete understanding of one's subject, the difficulties of dealing with written information and with facts or hunches that somehow refuse to "fit into" an emerging draft, the writer's desire to be seen as a person of good sense and goodwill, and the literal presence of the person being written about. This is writing which matters, in ways that everyone understands. I invite the group to introduce and explore such issues orally, in general terms; we explore them in greater particularity and depth in students' accompanying letters and my responses.

Our assignments are open-ended; unlike the sketch of a classmate, few of them specify subjects, and most stem fairly directly from personal experience. With Moffett (1992), I see writing as abstracted *from* experience, for some purpose or other. We shape experiences differently, and frequently it is in the shaping that we discover new potentials yet to be explored. *In my writing I see experiences being lived out on paper. My writing is talking to me. I feel like there is a conversation going on inside of me. I can write what I want to.* The intimacy of writing groups helps us sense those potentials and to experience the satisfaction and support of human response to the texts of their writing and the textures of their lives.

When there is time and after we have begun to become comfortable with our own writing, we read essays by published authors. Students choose these and lead our discussions of them. As we read, I ask that we consider two questions: What draws your interest, focuses your attention? What features and qualities of the text lead your interest to be focused in that way, rather than some other? Seeing such shapings at work is often easier in someone else's text than in one's own, although I hope that the reading will help students begin to see their own texts differently. In any case, I am inviting students to become reflective of their own reading; they frequently report, to my surprise, that for them this is a new way *of* reading. *I [am learning] to read between the lines, in the margins, through the words, into the language, and wherever else it requires me to find a language that I can relate to and see exactly what the author intended by the language that he or she used. [It seems that] my eyes have just opened and seen a new world.*

We keep a daily journal—just ten minutes or so of jotting— every day. Subjects and approaches are completely open, and students know that I will not see any entries they do not want me to see. The aim initially is fluency, followed by experimentation and exploration. Accompanying each entry is a very brief "composing observation," recording whatever the writer has noticed about the composing or the text of that particular entry and serving as a brief reflection on that writing. *[The journal] has shown me how to loosen my thoughts and begin to make sense out of infant ideas. [My] writing critic needed to be turned off long enough to explore an idea fully. / My journal showed me how diverse my mind really is. I would often start out on one topic, but find that I had ended up on something almost totally different, yet connected in some way through my mind's eye. The writing showed me that thinking process./ My journal entries seem to be me talking to you and thinking to you. I guess they are really me talking to myself.*

Around midterm, I often invite students to shift the directions of these daily writings, using whatever form(s) of writing they wish where the writing's purpose is to help them improve their mastery of materials in some other course they are taking. I want students to experience what I can never effect in lecture: that our learning becomes more confident and deeper when what we are learning becomes more than information to be stored in memory, when instead we represent it to ourselves and thereby reflect upon it. *The journal has become a tool of discipline—I have come to realize that it is a valuable part in my daily process of understanding new ideas and developing old ones:*

> *I have learned that writing, itself, is an act of learning. The most profound thoughts that I have had this semester have come to me while I was scrawling madly, with pen and paper in hand. It is as if my mind starts to work as my pen begins to move across the page. By writing, I stimulate my own thinking process. If I can get the beginning of an idea on paper, I know that I can use my pen to pull the rest of it out of the corners of my brain. In the same way, I can coerce an idea out of its hiding place by talking through it with another person.*
>
> *I think the [journal writing] quality was best when I was writing and trying to explain something to myself—when there was a search for meaning, even if I didn't come to any near-divine revelations. By writing things down, I could see how I think. I can go back and follow the associative algorithms in the thinking process.*
>
> *Since midterm, I see how beneficial my writing has become in my other classes. I remember thinking, "How will writing help me in accounting or microeconomics or my computer class?" Now, I wonder how I ever got by without it! I guess I was doing just that—getting by. I have noticed an overwhelming difference in all my classes. Even if my actual grade hasn't improved, I believe I am actively learning the material instead of just memorizing it. I am even participating more in class—probably because I am much more interested now.*
>
> *I do the "writing as I read" routine in Eastern Religion class. Had great success so far. Even now, with the study of the myths of Hinduism, they are very complex. Yet, as I read and write, the main points clarify for me. I get lazy and do not want to take the time. Yet I know unless I do, I will miss out so much. And, I notice about 1 per cent of students doing this. One even shrieked at me, "Why do you write SO much?" I answered, "Because I want REALLY to learn this." She didn't understand, I know. It's too bad, too.*
>
> *Once I got past the stage in all my writing of seeing it as something that was going to influence my final grade, I really started getting somewhere. [My writing] has taught me that I can learn from myself. I have always*

insisted that my learning has to come from someone who knows what they are doing. And I do have a lot of things to learn from other people but once I get inside myself I can learn a hell of a lot that I didn't even think about before. What I am trying to say and could say if it weren't for all these words, is that this class for me is as much about the actual thinking process as it is about the writing.

One thing I did was to take a single line or thought out of my notes and then write a whole page stemming from that initial idea or concept. This was interesting because it let my mind wander through [related matters]. By the time I had muddled my way through a page of such an entry, I began to develop a deeper realization and understanding of that one sentence or idea. It had become attached to me because I had connected it to my own thinking, giving it a corner in my mind. Concepts that I dealt with seemed to lose their abstractness and take on a fuller and more aware meaning.

I had always thought that the more I learned, the better I could write, but now it seems that the more I write, the better I learn the material.

Students should experience their writing as something they can do, which can sustain them as human beings and can open to them as learners the potentials of new insights. They should, in other words, experience their writing as a reflective medium. *I started seeing how surprisingly insightful some of my thoughts were, and I then had the confidence to move on. I honestly believe that if I hadn't been "responding" to my own responses, I'd have never even known what my thoughts were.*

For us, letters are the initial and essential medium for students' reflections. Students tell me that they look forward to mine, and I enjoy writing to them. However, the really important letters, of course, are the ones the students write to me and, really, to themselves. *[My letters] give me traction when I write. I was talking to one of your former students who said that when she gets stuck on an assignment, or can't get her ideas clear, she writes a Dear Sam letter, and it gets her unstuck. She gets that traction you spoke of earlier in the semester.* It is in the letters that students are most likely to begin experiencing their writing as a reflective medium. *I remember sitting in front of that blank piece of paper wondering how on earth I could get something written. It turns out, that blank piece of paper was really my mind because I wasn't really thinking at all. I sure wish I'd known how much more effective I could be!* To engage in the experience of reflection, I believe, is to lead an active life of the mind. Absent such a life, much of what we do educationally is waste and void.

OUTCOMES: IN DIALOGUE WITH . . .

> Several days ago I wrote in my daybook that personal experience is everyone's pundit—a basis and source for opinion. . . . Does that make sense?
> —*A recent letter from Greg Hathaway, a writing student from several years ago*

"Does that make sense?" Such a question, which I often read in a student's letter at some point in the semester, suggests that the student's commitment is to make meaning, rather than just to fill the form of some assignment. More importantly, it usually signals that student's turn to reflection of a new sort: a relationship between the person and the writing has become promising in new ways. The writing is no longer circumscribed by what, for that student, is the positive, is the factual, is demonstrably (and often trivially) "true." Instead, the writing is arising from some place(s) closer to the outer edges of that student's consciousness. It is serving as a probe moving that person toward potentials yet to be grasped, ideas in the making. Such a shift brings with it the student's expression of a new uncertainty about the writing itself. The text suddenly seems problematic in some sense; it seems much less solid, it is seen more as a fluid medium. The writing has become, I would say, a medium of reflection; and a property of a reflective medium, whether it is a mirror or the surface of a still pond, is that it calls attention away from its surfaces, toward some depth. That is what makes the medium reflective.

"Does that make sense?" The turn signaled by that question almost always brings a second consequence: The writing is far better than anything I have previously seen by that student. It is substantial in some new way; it reflects and extends the student's thinking, and so it challenges mine.

The recent letter from Greg Hathaway illustrates one shape his own thinking has assumed:

> *The process of writing as I see it is certainly not limited to the boundaries of putting pen to paper. It is situated in a humanistic, social context which, as you have said, "shapes and constrains both the act of writing and the text(s) produced." I see these ideas taking shape in my own writing. My process stems from my own context, my own experience. Several days ago I wrote in my daybook that personal experience is everyone's pundit—a basis and source for opinion. So for me, my context slants my writing in its own unique way. This idea is familiar to both of us but what is more interesting is how reflecting on how I write (my process) affects how I see my context. In dissecting my process I am forced to honestly view how I remembered, how I*

related those reflections, how I viewed a particular situation at the time I gave words to it. Because the dissecting is subsequent to the initial response of an event through writing, my cognitive ability to understand the response is less inclined to be hampered by the emotion of that preceding event when I review my process. Does that make sense? So it seems [that just] as writing illuminates our "frame of reference" to ourselves, the succeeding look at how we write can show us why and how we frame our views.

Greg is seeing his texts in relation to something beyond themselves, a dynamic I would hope for all students; the writing has become a medium of reflecting. For Greg, the writing is deepening his understanding of both the context in which he is doing it and his own framework from within which the writing arises.

Those discoveries are Greg's; not many students would be as insightful or would articulate just the same discoveries. However, in many students, I see something like the following progression through the semester: Initially, their writing is a performance to be assessed (and usually found wanting) against someone else's standards that are external and apparently arbitrary. They then find themselves in dialogue with me and other classmates—dialogue that certainly informs and in some measure sustains their composing of texts. Later, the crucial dialogue comes to be one they carry on with themselves and with some aspect(s) of the world around them, including subjects they are trying to master. The text, as well as any accompanying reflection, has become a medium of reflection. At that point, the student has become an independent writer, an independent learner.

In course grades, I intend to reward independence. As part of an initial "course rationale," students have received this characterization of "A" work in our course:

> Independent learning taking place with some consistency; the student's language (especially in writing but also orally) shows that her/his language is becoming important in that learning. A few signs (not an exhaustive list) of "A" work: a variety of strategies tried and commented on in daily writings; insightful observations and questions on writing, in daily writing and submitted work; engagement over time with questions about writing (ones the student raises or ones I raise in conversational responses); coming back to earlier thoughts to extend or qualify them; submitted writing that often has something of substance to say and says it with some clarity and purpose; thoughtful engagement with other students, orally and in writing. *"A" learners are curious persons.*

Similar paragraphs accompany my characterization of other grading points: "B" learners are perplexed persons, who have not quite decided whether to become "curious" or "complacent" or who haven't quite found ways to become either. "C" learners are complacent persons. "D" learners are uninvolved persons. "F" students are people who have failed themselves, by not showing up or not doing the assigned work.

Reminded of those deliberately general guidelines, students write an extended reflection on their work at midterm and again at the end of the course. Within the parameters of our guidelines, they are invited (though not required) to propose a grade for themselves, in light of standards they essentially set for themselves. In any case, the student's reflection allows me in some measure to read and review that student's work through her or his own eyes. The resulting grades are a matter of responsible judgment, rather than abdication to some external standards; I feel confident of these grades' accuracy and justice. Guided by students' reflections, the grading process is also a time for me to reflect and to keep those passages that will deserve further thought in the future.

CONCLUSIONS

Is this approach effective with all students? No. For some, writing remains a performance for the teacher, and their accompanying letters remain perfunctory; they never establish the dialogue(s) on whose basis deeper learning could occur. My approach rests on the assumption that what we are prepared to ask signals what we are prepared to learn, and that is not a true assumption for all students. Some students, if their writing is generally competent, exit my course with a "C" grade and with their writing pretty much unchanged. I can only hope that something may have taken root that will grow after our course is done; there are times when we teachers need to sustain ourselves with such hopes. *We don't change 21-year-old habits and tendencies in 3 months. Instead, what we try to do is open our ears and listen. Having listened, read, and discussed, we then go home and try to write. We place our pens on the first line of the page, open a direct channel between our minds and our fingers, and let nature take its course. This is the beginning.*

Is this approach the best one for any student? I believe so, but I have reservations. It is merely the best way that I can teach, and I deeply honor colleagues who teach differently and quite possibly better than I do. Our aim, I am convinced, is the same. We want to develop students whose writing is a thoughtful medium of judgment and decision, a guide to responsible action. Such writing requires reflection, but the best way to develop reflection may not be to attend to it as directly as my courses do. Polanyi's "tacit understanding," for instance, is not at work only with students of Polanyi. It is at work with all of us, including those for whom the tacit remains, well, tacit.

Recently a superb former student visited my current class. Kathy Hoyle and I had been together for both semesters of her freshman English, several years ago. I asked her whether there has been any lasting influence for her from our work together. "I can voice myself now," she replied. She went on to say that she takes risks with her writing now, and she seeks professors' permission to complete assigned projects in novel ways. She also has become impatient with instruction that seems not to respect her own engagement with the subject. For that reason, in fact, she has transferred to a smaller school.

"I never could figure just what you wanted in a paper." That comment, which I frequently hear after a course is finished, is one that more engaged students clearly intend as a compliment, rather than a complaint. *I appreciate your recognition of the fact that vagueness brings possibly more creativeness than does exactness in instruction. I wish that more professors and school teachers understood that less instruction can prove more successful than specifics and rules. The directions they give make them feel confident that the student will return a paper with the information they want. What they don't seem to realize is that the less strict their instructions are, the more imaginative and personally reflective the papers will be. They will show what the student knows, not what a book told them.* Even with the best students, however, a semester is so short that there are valuable places where our approach seldom gets us. We seldom attend much, explicitly, to issues of argument or of academic writing; the more intimate dialogues prove so new and so enticing that it can become difficult to move students into dialogue with the wider world, including the school subjects in which the academy is mainly interested.

Would even the students who become engaged be better served by a more traditional approach, one focused more directly on teaching the features desired in particular genres of texts? In the short term, the answer is probably yes; more direct methods might well show more immediate results.

I mean to teach for a lifetime of learning, and writing, and reflecting. *Pushing me into the pool of language [has made me] a different person.* The goal is different from teaching for some test, no matter how wisely constructed, or for superior performance on the next paper, in the next semester.

Still, I have reservations. I think of high school seniors, students of a former student of mine. She reports that they went off to college, eager to lead a life of the mind. However, they came back disillusioned, unable to find anyone there, student or faculty, who shared that interest. Those students haunt me. So does Kathy Hoyle.

Is higher education as intellectually barren as their experience suggests? I hope it is not, and I believe it need not be. I see intellectually engaged students flourish, even in terms of traditional grades. I talk with faculty colleagues, who are in the midst of interesting ideas. However, students seem too seldom to *see* these interests, these ideas. Lectures are fact-focused instead, and students' academic reading is often restricted to textbooks, perhaps the most singularly *un*reflective genre of writing known to humankind. In our institutional life, any reflective dimension is so thoroughly tacit as to be invisible to many students.

Our course, which I tell students should be an island of sanity in a world which may seem to have lost its mind, is a beginning in another direction. *I have become more objective without losing my right to subjectivity.* Sometimes, in the reflective discussions our class has at the end of the semester, I hear students say that they now understand my course rationale in ways they could not several months earlier. Frequently they add, "Now we are ready to begin." For each of us, that is the best for which I can hope.

REFERENCES

Aristotle. (1941). The rhetoric. W. Rhys Roberts (Trans.). In R. McKeon (Ed.), *The basic works of Aristotle* (pp. 1317–1451). New York: Random House.

Booth, W. C. (1974). *Modern dogma and the rhetoric of assent*. Chicago: The University of Chicago Press.

Elbow, P. (1973). *Writing without teachers*. London: Oxford University Press.

Elbow, P., Emig, J., Phelps, L., Wallace, E., & Watson, S. (1990-1991). Polanyian perspectives on the teaching of literature and composition. *Tradition and Discovery, 17*(1/2), 4-17.

Eliot, T. S. (1962). Burnt Norton. In *The Complete Poems and Plays, 1909-1950* (pp. 117–122). New York: Harcourt, Brace, and World.

Gelwick, R. (1977). *The way of discovery: An introduction to the thought of Michael Polanyi*. New York: Oxford University Press.

Miller, D. L. (1986). *The question of the Book: Religion as texture*. Charlotte: Department of Religious Studies, UNC Charlotte.

Moffett, J. (1965). I, you, and it. In *Active voice: A writing program across the curriculum* (2nd ed., pp. 196–203). Portsmouth, NH: Boynton/Cook.

Pirsig, R. (1975). *Zen and the art of motorcycle maintenance*. Toronto: Bantam.

Polanyi, M. (1964a). *Personal knowledge: Towards a post critical philosophy.* New York: Harper.

Polanyi, M. (1964b). *Science, faith, and society* (2nd ed.). Chicago: The University of Chicago Press.

Polanyi, M. (1969). (1969). *Knowing and being* (M. Grene, ed.). Chicago: The University of Chicago Press.

Poteat, W. H. (1985). *Polanyian meditations: In search of a post-critical logic.* Durham: Duke University Press.

Poteat, W. H. (1990). *A philosophical daybook: Post-critical investigations.* Columbia: University of Missouri Press.

Poteat, W. H. (1994). *Recovering the ground: A philosophical essay in recollection.* Albany: State University of New York Press.

Prosch, H. (1986). *Michael Polanyi: A critical exposition.* Albany: State University of New York Press.

Schön, D. A. (1983). *The reflective practitioner: How professionals think in action.* New York: Basic Books.

Schön, D. A. (1987). *Educating the reflective practitioner: Toward a new design for teaching and learning in the professions.* San Francisco: Jossey-Bass.

Schön, D. A. (1991). *The reflective turn: Case studies in and on educational practice.* New York: Teachers College Press.

Scott, D. (1985). *Everyman revisited: The common sense of Michael Polanyi.* Lewes, Sussex, England: The Book Guild Limited.

Stock, P. L. (1995). *The dialogic curriculum: Teaching and learning in a multicultural society.* Portsmouth, NH: Boynton/Cook.

Watson, S. D., Jr. (1973). *Michael Polanyi and the recovery of rhetoric.* Unpublished doctoral dissertation, University of Iowa.

Watson, S. D., Jr. (1981a). Polanyi and the contexts of composing. In A. Freedman & I. Pringle (Eds.), *Reinventing the rhetorical tradition* (pp. 19-26). Urbana, IL: National Council of Teachers of English.

Watson, S. D., Jr. (Ed.). (1981b). [Special double issue on Michael Polanyi]. *Pre/Text: An Inter-Disciplinary Journal of Rhetoric, 2*(1/2).

Watson, S. D., Jr. (1981). Polanyi's epistemology of Good Reasons. In R. McKerrow (Ed.), *Explorations in rhetoric: Studies in honor of Douglas Ehninger* (pp. 49-68). Dallas: Scott, Foresman.

Watson, S. D., Jr. (1990). Letters on writing: A medium of exchange with students of writing. In K. Adams (Ed.), *Teaching advanced composition: Why and how* (pp. 133-150). Portsmouth, NH: Heinemann.

White, J. B. (1984). *When words lose their meaning: Constitutions and reconstitutions of language, character, and community.* Chicago: The University of Chicago Press.

6 REVISION AS SELF-ASSESSMENT

Richard L. Larson

Lehman College of The City University of New York

For the last 30 or so years (from the time I entered the profession of the teaching of writing as my chosen specialty within the teaching of English), the revision of a writer's work has been a central emphasis in courses on writing. "Writing," various teachers (including me) have at times intoned in conferences, "is revision." Others have put it this way: "Learning to write" (or strengthening one's ability to write) "is learning to revise." Those who emphasize revision have called attention to the etymology of the term: to see again. The writer who revises conscientiously has to see the subject, and the writer's own draft, again anew through fresh eyes. Revision, teachers have proclaimed, is not the same as editing; in editing, one corrects errors, eliminates minor infelicities of style, and perhaps removes unnecessary words. But in revising one looks again at the subject, reconsiders one's approach to the subject, and determines whether one's approach, one's ideas, one's data, meet the needs of the "rhetorical situation" in which the writer is addressing a reader directly, to help resolve what has been called the "exigency" that is evoking the writing. This discussion deals with "addressed" writing; it does not deal with writing as personal exploration that is not addressed to a reader or readers. Nor does it deal significantly with writing that mainly analyzes a written text, the writer's own or another person's.

This act of reseeing a subject, a body of data, a draft text, when it is performed deliberately and advisedly, is fundamentally an act of assessment, although students and teachers typically do not discuss or view it as such. The reviser ideally examines what is already in place on the page against some conception of what the experience of reading that page ought to feel like—that is, against a "criterion" or "criteria." For many writers, however, these criteria seem dimly glimpsed, unarticulated, intuitive. (This may be the reason why, for many writers, revision consists of changing words and idioms to those that "sound" better.) Nonetheless, the act of appraising an object, a text, a phenomenon against a standard is the essence of assessment: It determines the worth of that which is examined. If a student is assessed by means of a test, the tester has a set of criteria that the student is expected to meet: The details of a student's performance are compared with the details of what those with the power of judgment have decided that they expect of the student.

Revision of a text, therefore, reflects or ought to reflect the fruits of an act of assessment. However, often it is the teacher's assessment, or perhaps a peer's assessment, that the writer responds to, sometimes without agreeing with, or "buying," that assessment. When the teacher of writing, in the role of reader, directs that a text be altered, or suggests how it might be altered, or records a response to that text which implies to a (conscientious, or apprehensive) student—a student who wants to do well, or to one who fears doing less well—that the text falls short, the student may wish, or be forced, to revise. One task of the teacher, then, is to wean the student from unexamined dependence on another person's assessment—to help the student become an autonomous reviser, that is, to help the student recognize how to revise, and become concerned about the works that he or she wants to revise. That is, the teacher is responsible for helping the student understand how to revise a text, helping the student to read the text with the eye of the teacher, or, better, helping the student read with the eye of the reader whom the writer is addressing. One task of the teacher is to promote in students the willingness, and the ability, to engage in informed self-assessment. Only by engaging in such informed self-assessment can the writer hope to establish and enact his or her independence from the teacher and become a self-directing writer fully responsible for her own text (see Flower et al., 1986; Murray, 1980.)

Thus baldly stated, the linkage between revision and self-assessment seems obvious. The devil, however, is in the details: the details of the metacognitive processes by which a writer comes to perceive the desirability of making changes in a text. By what metacognitive processes does the student come to understand how to constructively "read" a text of his or her own? Learning that art means learning to decenter, to step outside of one's intentions in a draft text and read that text with the eye of another, the eye of the intended reader. That learning includes the writer's recognizing what operations of mind he or she activates in order to reach an assessment decision. For the writer, it is the kind of reading that is at the heart of self-assessment. It is that kind of reading which is the central stimulus to revision.

Where do the difficulties in self-assessment lie for the writer? Why is perceptive revision for many writers such a difficult process? Why is informed self-assessment so hard to achieve? The answer has at least two parts. First, many writers (not just students, but writers of all kinds) have acute difficulty bringing themselves to look, in their imaginations, through the eyes of another person at a text that they have created. (This is not to disparage students as readers; even as I write these words I am not sure I can anticipate how a reader confronting this chapter in the context of other works on self-assessment might see it.) In my Advanced Exposition and report writing classes, I stress from the start of the semester the need for students to try to look at their drafts through the eyes of a reader other than themselves—for instance, through the eyes of another participant in an argument or through those of an executive receiving a report that, let's say, the executive has not asked for, or even a report that she *has* asked for. (What information, given in what detail, and at what length, with what commentary, will that executive be prepared to receive?) To begin answering such questions, the writer *creates* his or her reader. Even after receiving regular reminders of the need to step outside themselves as they read their drafts, however, few students reveal the ability to do so, maybe because they do not know what it feels like to do so. Receiving peers' or teachers' comments is no substitute for imagining the possible responses of a "created reader." Among other judgments the writer must make is whether the text is going to be accessible, comprehensible to the intended/imagined reader. What, the writer might ask, does the reader know about the subject? What background does he or she bring to the text that will enable him or her to deal with the subject and the writer's assertions? What does the reader expect to see?

A second reason that writers have trouble assessing their own drafts is that writers by and large do not know enough about how texts work. That is to say, they have little experience in relating a reader's possible or imaginable responses to the specific characteristics of that text. To be sure, students can often give perceptive responses to draft texts even without a knowledge of the workings of discourse; they can often give fellow students wise guidance toward revision of their fellows' texts, because they are looking at language structures they did not create. However, the assessment of one's own texts is harder, precisely because the student writer is not accustomed to looking at his or her own texts with the eye of another reader. Some familiarity with how discourse works can equip the student for self-assessment by offering some probes with which to look at his or her own texts. I mention here just a few such probes—"heuristics," if you will—that the writer engaged in self-assessment may find useful to apply. These probes may give the writer a few beginners' tools for judging their work with an eye toward revision.

Consider first a probe for appraising the writer's consistency in treating her subject. Writing teachers have, broadly speaking, understood that at the start of a piece of writing a writer inevitably creates expectations in a reader's mind about the writer's subject *and* approach to that subject (these matters are *not* the same as the writer's "thesis"). The writer, that is, forges a commitment to the reader about what the reader can expect in that writing. The reader can then test the writing by determining how well the writer has carried out his or her commitment to the reader. However, many student writers do not know about this concept; they do not have practice in sizing up the opening of a writing to locate the signals about why the writer is coming before the reader and what to expect as the writer proceeds. But the beginning of one's writing is an apt place to begin self-assessment looking toward revision. Unless the writer knows, or can guess, how beginnings work, that metacognitive act of self-assessment is not available to the writer. A related concept invites the self-assessing writer to view the text as raising (at the start) and answering (as the essay moves on) questions/issues for discussion. The writer can usefully probe how well he or she has answered the questions/resolved the issues introduced at the start, or even whether issues are raised at the start for which a reader can seek the answers later.

Similarly, the writer, in order to engage in informed self-assessment, leading perhaps to revision, will profit from having, metacognitively, a concept of "structure" and movement in a text. The writer gains from being able to identify major structural components of a piece of writing, and from knowing how to describe the pattern or sequence they follow as the piece unfolds. This does not mean that the writer needs to know the names of the common kinds of sequence that writers typically follow (these common kinds are the focus of many textbooks), or the principal patterns of reasoning as they might be taught in a course in thought and argument. However, the writer does need to be able to locate where the arrangement of subjects in his or her draft essay does not make clear the connections among those subjects, and why the connections break down (if they do). In order to assess the wisdom of the structure in the draft, the writer needs to be able to say, for instance, looking at the draft with a reader's eye, "The reader will not be able to tell clearly why point B follows point A or why point C follows point B." If B is an example of an assertion made as point A, and C is a qualification of A, the writer needs to be able to see the structure, and to test whether a reader not privy to the writer's ideas can identify what is going on. To be sure, the writer engaging in self-assessment may feel a "dissonance," a discomfort, at a sequence of thought without knowing why the discomfort is felt. But informed self-assessment—self-assessment that can lead to revision—ordinarily requires the ability to employ knowledge about how "structures" in texts work, if the writer is to be able to revise.

The writer engaging in self-assessment can also profit from introductory familiarity with how data can be used and should be used—with the value of data in supporting general assertions and in leading a reader to believe a statement. If the writer is going to assess the relevance (to his or her subject) and the cogency of one or more statements, that writer needs to know, metacognitively, how statements are made relevant and cogent for the reader. The writer not accustomed to questioning the adequacy of his or her data is less likely to reach perceptive self-assessment than one who has had such practice. This habit of questioning the value of information leads to the regular asking of such questions as, "How do I know this?" "Why do I believe this?" "Must this general statement be qualified?" "Is that person or source entitled to be trusted or believed?" Important questions about data also touch what is taken for granted in, and what is implied by, an assertion: "What am I assuming to be true here?" "Will my reader believe and accept what I am assuming?" "To what other views or beliefs does my statement here seem to commit me?" The habit of asking such questions, and other similar ones, is a habit of mind that has come to be labeled "critical thinking." This habit of mind does not necessarily imply (as the term "critical" might suggest) a refusal to believe; it can refer equally to the willingness to build a sound framework for believing or a sound justification for belief. Developing this inclination of mind, however, and practicing it regularly on one's own assertions (not just those of others) is an essential step in learning conscientious and productive self-assessment.

A further qualification for effective self-assessment (the kind that enables revision) is at least some knowledge of how sentences work. This is not a recommendation that students be taught directly at length the grammar of English; it is not a reaffirmation of the concern for "correctness" of syntax and inflection of nouns, pronouns, and verbs. It is a suggestion that ability at self-assessment includes the ability to see what one's sentences are "saying" by the way in which they are put together. Particularly valuable is a familiarity with what might be called the logic of coordination and subordination: What do "parallel" structures signify? When are they appropriate? When are they misleading? What do various kinds of subordinate structures in syntax express? The writer who knows the semantic force of relative clauses and of causal structures, including clauses beginning with "since," "because," "due to," "thus," "therefore"; of conditional structures ("if . . . then . . . "); of concessive structures ("although," "despite"); of qualification and reaffirmation ("except for . . . nevertheless . . . ") is in a much better position to determine the force of her sentences and recognize the need for changing those sentences than one who does not have such a sense of syntax. It has been my experience in teaching such activities as editing that students often do not have a clear sense of how their sentences express meanings by the structures in which they are cast.

One could no doubt add other probes that a writer can employ in looking at his or her texts. One could identify word choice as a separate focus of self-assessment. However, studies of revision have suggested that students often spend a good deal of time changing words or idioms, but not much time on the matters I've enumerated (see Sommers, 1980). Those foci mentioned here give the student a beginning toward the assessment of substance, structure, and language in draft texts.

Using these probes, of course, has to be taught; most writers do not practice the use of such probes unless the writers have been helped to understand them and how they work. That teaching needs, in my view, to be fairly direct; students need to learn the concepts I've enumerated. One way to teach the concepts is to present students with a variety of texts and invite them to examine each with the aid of the probes mentioned. These probes can be named and explained, and students can be directly urged to apply them. Then, with the aid of members of the class, students can be guided in applying these probes to examples of their own writing, so that they become familiar with these processes of self-assessment and how the processes play out—how they sound—in use.

Asking students to practice applying evaluative questions to their texts and fellow students' texts, of course, is nothing new. Many teachers follow that practice. However, the probes suggested here are often not among those that students are invited to practice, even though the areas discussed are central to the workings of text, much more central than some of the editorial concerns that are often heavily taught. One can suggest that students need to be aware of, and look at, the "principal features" that are likely to make the greatest impact on another person's reception of the text. Writing is a social activity practiced in a context of human relationships. Unless the writer is composing a poem or story where the main theme and internal structure of language are what determine the effectiveness of the text, the writer's assessment of his or her own work needs to focus on how the text will work in that context.

A writer's self-assessment must imagine the social situation in which a text emerges. The process is incomplete and unreliable if it does not relate writing to its rhetorical/social setting. Self-assessment is a rhetorical act.

REFERENCES

Flower, L., et al. (1986). Detection, diagnosis, and the strategies of revision. *CCC, 37*, 16–55.

Murray, D. (1980). Internal revision: A process of discovery. In C. Cooper & L. Odell (Eds.), *Research on composing: Points of departure*. Urbana, IL: National Council of Teachers of English.

Sommers, N. (1980). Revision strategies of student writers and experienced adult writers. *CCC, 31*, 378–387.

REFERENCES

7 FREEWRITING IN THE MIDDLE: SELF-HELP FOR COLLEGE WRITERS ACROSS THE CURRICULUM

Vicki Tolar Collins

Oregon State University

I am so overwhelmed by all the information I've found that I don't know what to do. There were 111 articles listed on the CD-rom index, and hundreds of books in the online catalog. How do people make sense of this stuff? Maybe I'd better just drop the course.

I'm fed up with this project. The teacher made it too complicated. The stupid library never has the books or journals I need. How can I be expected to do this? Oh well, I've done the best I can.

For many college writers facing a deadline on a major course project, the moment when they feel most alone and most unsupported in their writing process, the moment when they would most like to walk away from the whole academic scene, is that dangerous threshold between data gathering and synthesis, that precarious time between undigested notes and well-developed draft. In this liminal period shortly before a project draft is due, students often feel overwhelmed and underprepared as thinkers, as writers, and as aspiring participants in the disciplinary conversation. Because little attention has been directed toward this critical time in the writing of a major project, it is a site of composing that merits attention from teachers of writing.

My research suggests that teachers across the curriculum can help frustrated students become purposeful writers who are motivated and able to move forward with their composing to complete the project at hand. The method of transformation discussed in this chapter is a self-assessment heuristic or exercise in which students freewrite in response to five questions designed to help them develop a plan for drafting and move the writing forward. I designed this exercise with the belief that by freewriting in the middle, students learn to step back from the overwhelming data or unsatisfying draft, assess where they actually are in the project, identify major problems or blocks, and draw on their own past successes and personal capabilities to take responsibility for solving remaining problems.

Unlike most freewriting strategies, which are directed at the prewriting/invention stage of writing, and unlike most self-assessment strategies, which focus on a completed written product, freewriting in the middle gives students an opportunity to discover a path out of whatever writing wilderness they have encountered or created. Because students' self-assessments become illuminating snapshots of where the class members are in their writing projects, teachers benefit from the exercise as well. They can address common problems, support individual writers, and make needed revisions in the assignment for future use. My goal in this chapter is to describe the problem-solving exercise I call "freewriting in the middle," explain its roots in composition pedagogy and cognitive psychology, present results of a study of student responses to the exercise, and identify the usefulness of freewriting in the middle for writers and teachers across the curriculum.

THE EXERCISE AND ITS CLASSROOM USE

Freewriting in the middle is a form self-assessment that disrupts expectations about freewriting and about self-assessment. I have structured this exercise so that students freewrite about their writing process rather than their topic, they freewrite in the middle of the project rather than at the beginning, and they freewrite to assess their process rather than to generate ideas about their topic. Self-assessment focuses on process in progress rather than completed text.

The exercise is most useful as an in-class assignment performed about a week before a draft of the project is due. At that point students have probably begun work on the project but may have encountered problems or roadblocks in their research and/or writing. With only a week to go, even procrastinators are feeling the pressure. They need to get moving on the assignment but may not know how. The exercise is structured so that students do not necessarily have to be experienced at freewriting to benefit from it. What exactly does the exercise involve?

The teacher gives these instructions to the class:

This is an exercise which will help you make progress on your project using freewriting. That means you should let your ideas and your writing flow freely without worrying about spelling or punctuation or even writing in sentences. The purpose is to help you learn more about where you are on your project. I will redirect your freewriting about every 2 minutes. Try to keep writing without stopping.

1. Write about where you are right now on your project. (2 minutes)
2. Now write about your major problem with the project at this moment. What is causing it? Describe the problem in as much detail as you can. (3 minutes)
3. Write about a time in the past when you had a similar problem and recall how you solved it. (2 minutes)
4. Write about what you can do to solve your major problem on this project. (2 minutes)
5. Now jot down a list of things you are going to do in order to complete the project on time. Remember that you need to complete a draft by _____ . (2 minutes)

The first question in the exercise encourages self-awareness, helping students become fully conscious of where they are on their project by inviting them to describe what they have (and have not) done. The second question asks them to make an evaluative decision about what is blocking the way in the writing project. Naming a problem makes it real and can be the first step toward solving it. The third question invites students to make connections between past writing experiences and the problems they are now encountering: Can knowledge gained through previous experience (positive or negative) help in the present dilemma? The fourth question asks students to formulate a solution, to take responsibility for their own writing. The last question extends the problem solution into a proactive "To Do" list and reemphasizes the limited time remaining before the due date.

THEORETICAL ROOTS OF FREEWRITING IN THE MIDDLE

From a theoretical standpoint, freewriting in the middle is a mix of Elbow's (1981) self-exploratory expressivism and the cognitive problem-solving strategies of Flower and Hayes (1981). The directed freewrite grows out of Macrorie's (1968) early notions of writing freely to see what emerges and Elbow's (Elbow & Belanoff, 1989) expressive notion of freewriting, which he describes as "Private nonstop writing where you write about whatever you want to write about or put down whatever comes to mind. . . . Don't worry about whether your writing is any good, or even whether it makes sense. . . . Try to follow the writing where it goes" (p. 9). Freewriting in the middle is an extension of focused freewriting, where students stay with one topic during the exercise (Elbow & Belanoff, 1989), but may seem even more directive and goal-oriented, and thus less "free," because specific questions are used. The goal is not to generate text that might become part of a larger piece of writing; rather, the goal is to think and write about the writing process. Unlike Elbow and Belanoff's process journal questions, which usually focus on completed texts, freewriting in the middle is a way to find direction in the midst of writing.

The problem-solving aspect of the exercise is rooted in the work of Flower and Hayes on cognition in composing. Flower and Hayes's studies using think-aloud protocols characterize writers as constantly solving one problem or another. When Flower (1981) translated these cognitive theories into a writing textbook, *Problem-Solving Strategies for Writers*, she explained to student writers, "The goal of this book is to offer you a set of strategies for dealing with writing as a problem you can solve, and in so doing to give you more alternatives and more conscious control over your own writing" (p. 3). Flower's textbook includes numerous lists for self-reflection similar to the heuristic used in this study.

Freewriting in the middle combines a cognitive heuristic similar to Flower's with exploratory writing. The exploratory aspect of the exercise draws on student self-awareness and memory—perhaps a successful past experience with writing—and gives the writer space and time for imagining and planning behavioral change. The psychological roots of this approach can be seen in the work of cognitive psychologists like Albert Bandura, who believes that behavioral change is based as much on experiences of mastery as on symbolic representation. Bandura (1977a) suggested that transitory experiences leave lasting effects on the memory "by being coded and retained in symbols for memory representation" (p. 191). Furthermore, as cognitive psychologist R.C. Bolles (1972) indicated, individuals can generate self-motivation by cognitive representation of possible outcomes. Thus a student who thinks of a solution to his or her writing problem is motivated to pursue it to some extent simply by the cognitive representation of a positive outcome. (More recent applications of this theory occur in psychotherapeutic uses of visualization techniques.) Other studies in cognition reinforce the importance of goal setting and self-evaluation in behavior change (Bandura, 1976, 1977b).

A student can believe that a certain action will produce a specific outcome, but unless she also believes she is capable of performing the necessary action, her behavior will not be influenced by the causal knowledge, and she will not change. Bandura (1977a) said of self-efficacy, "Expectations of personal mastery affect both initiation and persistence of coping behaviors" (p. 193). I would suggest that assigning freewriting in the middle implies to students that the teacher believes they are each capable of solving their own writing problems and in fact helps them think of themselves as effective problem solvers, thus increasing their self-efficacy and the probability that they will have a successful outcome.

But does it work? A study based on use of the exercise in three classes provides insight.

DESIGN OF THE STUDY

Sixty-two college writers divided among three upper division writing-intensive courses in their major participated in the study. Each class was working on a different term project. The classroom teachers administered the exercise during class time about one week before a major due date on the term project. Students completed the exercise anonymously.

Group 1 was composed of 33 Animal Science majors taking a capstone writing-intensive course in beef production. Their major project was a collaborative assignment to update a 20-year-old State Extension Service publication on beef production for an audience of small cattle producers. In Group 2, numbering 11, majors varied, but they were primarily students in English as a Second Language (ESL) education. Group 2 was assigned to a collaborative project on Writing Across the Curriculum. (As a point of clarity, the students in this group were all native speakers of English preparing to teach English as a second language.) Group 3 was composed of 18 English majors in an upper division writing-intensive course in composition pedagogy. Their assignment was to prepare individual research projects on specific pedagogical approaches to the teaching of writing.

For the purposes of this chapter, I focus on questions two, three, and four in the freewriting exercise, thus looking at problems students identified, past memories they drew on, and solutions to their present problems.

RESULTS

Student Definitions of Writing Problems

The problems with the major projects were diverse, located both within and outside of the writer, and situated within the rhetorical and pedagogical context of specific assignments. Major problems (Question 2) identified by students can be grouped in the following categories, beginning with the most frequently mentioned category (see Table 7.1 for exact data):

1. *Cognitive problems*: finding a focus for the research, understanding the audience and its needs, selecting from an overwhelming amount of material, condensing information, writing succinctly, knowing how to evaluate data and information. (See Table 7.2)
2. *Time problems*: scheduling, hard to get the team together, too much to do, pressure from other classes, poor time management.
3. *Assignment problems*: too much busy work; assignment is too vague; assignment is too easy; assignment is not worthwhile; "We're having to do this [revise the publication] because some extension agent is too lazy to do it himself."
4. *Knowledge-base problems*: lack of knowledge about the topic; "I don't know enough about this to do the work;" lack of knowledge of how to update terminology and information.
5. *Relational/collaboration problems*: worry about how the group will work together; worry about group participation; "I'm worried about how to tell my partner what I need."
6. *Victim problems*: the teacher made this too difficult; the library is poorly organized; the teacher lost my draft; feeling trapped by team; "I feel somewhat trapped because R. chose me. I felt like I could not say no in front of the class. She doesn't seem to be as interested or driven to do this as I am."
7. *Control problems*: anxiety about lack of control over the writing process in team effort because the writer is used to working alone; worry about the quality of the work produced by other team members; "I'm a person who likes to control those elements of my life that are controllable."

Table 7.1. Writing Problems Identified by Students (in Order of Frequency).

Type of Problem	Total n = 62	Class A Animal science n = 33	Class B ESL n = 11	Class C English n = 18
1. Cognitive (details in Table 7.2)	39	20	1	18
2. Time	13	6	5	2
3. Assignment	10	10	0	0
4. Knowledge base	8	5	1	2
5. Relational Collaboration	6	2	4	N/A
6. Victim	5	3	1	1
7. Loss of control	4	2	2	0
8. Attitude	3	3	0	0
9. Originality	3	0	0	3
10 Writing Skills	3	1	1	1
11. Emotional	2	0	1	1

Note. n = number of students participating. Some students identified more than one problem, so the total number of responses exceeds the number of participants.

Table 7.2. Cognitive Problems Identified by Writers.

Cognitive Problems	Total n = 39	Class A Animal science n = 20	Class B ESL n = 1	Class C English n = 18
1. Select and evaluate data; condense it	18	13	0	5
2. Understand audience	8	7	0	1
3. Find a focus	8	(Given)	1	7
4. Organize information	3	0	0	3
5. Document borrowed information	2	N/A	0	2

Note. n = number of students giving responses in this category.

8. *Attitude or priority problems*: boredom with the assignment or the class; self- indulgence; self-rationalization; "I'm ready to graduate;" "I feel like I have already paid my dues in this department;" "I know I should work on it this weekend, but I'm fly-fishing the Descheutes."

9. Originality problems: frustrated desire to bring something new to the discussion; awareness of depending too much on outside sources; "Where am I in this?"

10. Writing skills problems: "my writing style," lack of experience with teams; "I feel like one of Shaughnessy's basic writers."

11. Emotional problems: feeling overwhelmed; "The whole thing seems so big and important;" "I am wrung out academically."

Student Memories of Writing

The third question in the heuristic asked students to identify a time in the past when they had experienced a similar problem. Of the 62 students completing the exercise, only 4 stated that they were dealing with a problem they had never confronted before. Because student memories were individual and often idiosyncratic, it was not possible to count or exactly categorize each memory. However, there may be interest in some general accounting.

When asked how they had dealt with a similar problem in the past, nine students specifically mentioned a writing class as the context for previous experience, recalling these past solutions:

1. Staying up late to finish as a solution to procrastination.

2. Paying attention to audience: "I used to have the same problem (understanding audience needs) writing class papers. I decided to solve it by changing my style of writing and making better connections with people. I believe this to be a sign of maturity."

3. Eliminating irrelevant material and wordiness: "Writing term papers that are too long is the problem that I've had in the past. You write direct sentences and chop what doesn't need to be in the paper. With term papers it's easy to decide if something doesn't belong because the data won't or doesn't support [the thesis]."

4. "In [the earlier class] what I did was pushed myself and got the project done. I usually work best under pressure."

5. Eliminating redundancy: "When completing my senior thesis, I had too much information (much of which was

repetitive). But working with the professor, I found how
to combine and omit things . . . by taking the main points
of my section and combining a number of items together.
Lengthy explanations about uses and/or problems are not
essential."

Other students who did not refer directly to a writing class said they had
turned in the past to these solutions:

6. Rewriting.
7. Having others read the paper and give feedback.
8. Talking to people who might be like the audience.
9. Asking someone knowledgeable about the topic.
10. Doing more research.
11. Improving time management.
12. Telling themselves to "JUST DO SOMETHING."

Student Problem-Solving Strategies

After reflecting on past experiences, students were asked in Question 4 to
write about how they might solve their current problem. Sixty out of 62
writers offered a solution to their problems. They mentioned the
following approaches to resolving their project problems, beginning with
the most frequently mentioned solution (see Table 7.3 for exact data):

1. Ask for help (see Table 7.4):
   • Have others read my draft and suggest revision.
   • Ask for help from the teacher.
   • Talk or write to experts.
   • Ask for help from other group members.
   • Find a model.
2. Focus on the paper itself (see Table 7.5):
   • Focus on the paper as a whole; concentrate on one
     section.
   • Do more research; look at more sources.
   • Refine or revise over and over.
   • Break the problem down into steps and do one at a time.
   • Outline the paper.
   • Review the assignment sheet.
   • Ask myself questions about the audience's needs.
3. Set goals; manage time:
   • Set goals; prioritize what has to be done.
   • Organize my time between now and the due date.

4. Rely on self-motivation:
   - Positive self-talk: "Just do it!" "I need to get hold of myself"; "Relax and let my pen flow like some river out of my mind winding and coursing across my paper until it reaches the ocean of completeness." "I will be patient. I will get through this project."
   - Commitment to excellence: "Do my best"; "I want my form right."
5. Communicate needs to others:
   - "Tell team members what I need."
6. Be self-protective:
   - Self-care: "Preserve my sanity."
   - Fashion a self: "Commit myself to being cooperative, flexible with the group, in good humor; compromise with the group."
   - Compromise standards: "At this point I don't have enough time to really do an outstanding job on the rewrite."
7. Critique/attack the institution:
   - "Give my critique of the class to the professor."
   - "Tell someone the university should get rid of writing-intensive courses."
8. Avoid the problem:
   - Drop the course.
   - Avoid confrontation in the team by doing the other person's work.
   - Pay someone to do the work.
   - "Finish and forget it. Who cares?"
9. Stay up all night
10. Rely on past first-hand experience (for example, raising cattle for 16 years) rather than on the library sources. (The student's lived knowledge is at odds with sources.)
11. Do partner's work
12. Decide the problem can't be solved:
    - "No solution. We don't have enough time to work together. Everyone has different priorities."

DISCUSSION

The fact that advanced writers in this study were freewriting in the middle of actual long-term projects rather than responding to controlled laboratory prompts is both a strength and a limitation—a strength because the writing situation was not artificial, but a limitation because the three different assignments placed different demands on the writers.

Table 7.3. Solutions to Writing Problems (in order of frequency).

Solution	Total n = 62	Class A Animal science n = 33	Class B ESL n = 11	Class C English n = 18
1. Ask for help (details in Table 7.4)	26	14	6	6
2. Focus on the paper (details in Table 7.5)	25	8	5	12
3. Set goals, manage time	10	1	6	3
4. Self-motivate	7	5	1	1
5. Communicate needs to others	5	0	5	0
6. Protect self	4	0	3	1
7. Criticize teacher, library, or institution	4	4	0	0
8. Avoid problem	3	3	0	0
9. Stay up all night	1	1	0	0
10. Rely on own experience, not "experts"	1	1	0	0
11. Do partner's work	1	0	1	0
12. No solution	2	2	0	0

Note. n = number of students participating. Some students mentioned more than one solution, so the total number of solutions exceeds the number of participants.

Table 7.4. Solutions 1: Ask for Help.

Type of help wanted	Total n = 26	Class A Animal science n = 14	Class B ESL n = 6	Class C English n = 6
1. Have others read paper	11	7	1	3
2. Conference with teacher	7	2	3	2
3. Consult experts	6	4	2	0
4. Consult group member	1	1	0	0
5. Find a model	1	0	0	1

Note. n = number of participants giving responses in this category.

Table 7.5. Solutions 2: Focus on the Paper.

Area of focus	Total n = 25	Class A Animal science n = 8	Class B ESL n = 6	Class C English n = 11
1. Focus on paper as a whole or concentrate on one section	8	3	1	4
2. Do more research	7	2	3	2
3. Refine or revise over and over	4	0	0	4
4. Break paper into steps	3	2	1	0
5. Outline paper	2	0	1	1
6. Review assignment sheet	1	1	0	0

Note. n = number of participants giving responses in this category.

The potential for drawing exact comparisons and contrasts of writers across disciplines is also limited. For example, certain responses by the students in Animal Science appear more related to the nature of their assignment (to revise an existing brochure) than to the nature of student writers in Animal Science. Thus I hesitate to assert broad claims for what these data prove about advanced writers or about writers in a particular discipline. Rather, this study offers a counterpoint to the tidier, more structured studies conducted under controlled conditions with talk-aloud protocols and carefully coded responses, a counterpoint that may be less statistically valid, but in actuality is more similar to the classroom experiences of most student writers and their teachers. With the limitations is mind, certain overall observations can be made.

Much current scholarship on writing process assumes that problems of student writers are problems with writing. Although this sample of student responses indicates that some writers' problems are problems about writing, other problems are about other things: time (managing it, lack of it); collaboration and how to survive it; swirling emotions and need for control; attitudes toward assignments, toward teachers, and even attitudes toward "lazy" county extension agents. They are problems of relationship, of self-direction, of mind-set, of character, of life, reminding us that student writers have complicated lives, complicated schedules, varying levels of motivation, weary bodies and minds, and priorities for their own lives that often have nothing to do with how well the class is taught or how carefully the assignment is designed. Writing is not only imbedded in a rhetorical situation, it is also entangled in the complexity of a writer's life—entangled, therefore, in some matters that the teacher probably cannot engage or change.

However, as the data presented indicate, students *can* engage these matter and effect change. Writers can identify their own writing problems, make connections to past problems and successes, and imagine solutions. They can settle down, think, write, remember, connect, reflect, resolve, plan, set goals, prioritize. Although a few participating students did resist the self-assessment by blaming someone else for their problems, most students appeared to move through the exercise with energy and insight, indicating a willingness to take responsibility for their own writing and their own writing process.

It seems significant that only four students stated that they were encountering a problem for the first time. In the "problem" and "memory" statements, a number of students acknowledged the identified problem as a familiar recurring one, especially problems of time management and cognition. Remembering a past instance of success was positive, even for students with what might appear to be habitual problems. No student claimed total absence of past success. One student who did not recall past success wrote that during the exercise she had finally realized she did not have to keep repeating past mistakes.

The variety of problems most often encountered seems worthy of notice. Responses from the three classes suggest that many students experience at least some cognitive difficulty during a major project, particularly with selecting the best information on their topic from all available, evaluating what to use, and condensing it in their own text. Writers also struggle with understanding audience and finding a focus for their writing. These problems represent instructional needs that might not traditionally be addressed by teachers in various disciplines. But in fact, this knowledge (What counts as proof? Which sources are best? What does my audience need? What questions are worthy of study?) is usually discipline-specific and thus needs to be addressed when writing projects are assigned.

In an interesting way, the blaming some students did in their responses may be seen as socially constructed. For example, the resentful Animal Science major who attacks the beef brochure assignment because he believes the brochure should have been revised by the "lazy" extension agent might reflect prejudice of a farmer/rancher practitioner against the "expert" extension agent. Another way in which problems appear socially constructed emerged in the underlying belief of some Animal Science majors that in their major they should not be asked to do so much writing ("I am frustrated that a WIC course has taken over an animal science course. So that instead of learning new ideas in beef production we are doing busy work stuff . . ."). Students majoring in English and Education seemed to assume that heavy writing demands go with the territory, which is also a socially constructed assumption.

Because promoting self-efficacy was one goal of the assignment, it is important to observe whether students believed they could solve their problems. From time management, additional research, and improved communication to positive self-talk and commitment to excellence, most solutions suggest that the students believe they can take effective action to solve their problems. Only a few solutions (compromising standards, avoidance, feeling helpless, and blaming the institution) suggest lack of ability (or willingness) to solve the problem. These responses were isolated instances represented only 5 of 62 responses. Thus most students demonstrated what Bandura (1977a) would call "self-efficacy." When students wrote about how to resolve their present problems, many showed insight into their own writing processes and wrote in a tone of energetic commitment to change and action. They seemed able to give themselves the advice they needed, whether it was to communicate with their group members, calm down, or "Just do it!"

Responses also validate the use of freewriting as part of problem solving. It is a commonplace of psychotherapy that on some level the individual often knows the solutions to his or her own problems. Similarly, it is a commonplace of expressive approaches to composition that freewriting frees the writer to discover what he or she thinks and feels about a topic. Every student in the study articulated some notion of what he or she needed to do. Freewriting brought that knowledge to the writer's awareness and made it available for use.

No student complained of not knowing what freewriting was, indicating that the instructions to "let your ideas and your writing flow freely without worrying about spelling or punctuation or even writing in sentences" were adequate, even for those who might have been inexperienced with freewriting as a technique.

Benefits and Limitations for Students

Freewriting in the middle offers students both cognitive and affective gains. In the cognitive area, the exercise reminds students how much work remains to be done, invites them to name the problem impeding their work, encourages them to seek their own solution through memory and through logic, clarifies tasks by making them more concrete, provides impetus for goal setting and prioritizing. In addition, getting a "To Do" list down on paper can help students feel more organized and more in control of their work.

Furthermore, freewriting in the middle offers students affective gains in motivation and positive emotional orientation. By naming the problem, the writer sees its boundaries and thus may feel more able to solve it. One student said of the exercise, "It stopped my mind from swirling and calmed my panic." Other students reported a positive feeling from confronting fears through the freewrite, fears such as anxiety over a team member's contribution or anxiety about one's ability to carry through. One writer said, "I realized that my past problems don't have to be repeated." Another, sounding like a Nike commercial, wrote, "Just Do It! Just Do It! Just Do It!" Positive self-talk can be a powerful motivator. These positive affective outcomes contribute to the writer's sense of self-efficacy, the belief that the problem can be named and solved and the writing successfully completed. By freewriting in the middle of a project, student writers in any discipline can intervene in their own writing processes and even use the heuristic later as they encounter subsequent writing problems on this or another project.

However, what of the students who routinely plan and carry out their projects efficiently? Is this exercise a waste of their time? Maybe, maybe not. Of 62 students participating, 2 reported that they were on task and ahead of schedule, although one of them was still concerned about teammates who were not on schedule, writing:

> Cooperation is the only way to solve this problem. I'll have flexible hours and attempt to be patient—I will be patient. I intend to get through this project. I will do whatever is necessary to contribute to the collaborative effort in the best humor I can muster. In the future? Taking classes where I have a few, or at least one, buddy, someone I know well and like working with. Adapting to strangers' methods is somewhat unappealing to me.

This student was not only reinforcing his own determination to succeed, but also planning *beyond* the current assignment. As the saying goes, once burned, twice cautious. His positive self-talk seems helpful, even if it is not essential to his success in completing the project. If the majority of students are not perfectly organized and on schedule, the teacher seems justified in devoting 15 minutes of class time to problem solving.

Although an instructor could make the exercise optional, that may be counterproductive. Students may need self-reflection, but they probably won't choose it over early lunch or free time to hang out. If all students are asked to spend 15 minutes of class time in self-reflection on their writing process, the two students who are ahead may be bored, but the rest of their classmates are likely to be helped.

Another outcome that may be seen as both positive and negative is the experience of the extreme procrastinator who becomes anxious when she realizes how much work she has ahead. One student wrote, "I hoped the exercise would be helpful, but ended up feeling that it only makes me realize that I am way behind, that I can't catch up. I *think* I know what needs to be done, but I'm still a bit unclear. I want to be clear." For this student, the exercise produced negative affect and possibly even loss of self-efficacy if she is so far behind that she feels the task is impossible. She also wrote, "I do know that I need to sit down with my partner and decide how to proceed from here. What am I doing next, what is she doing next? How are we going to present this?" She may have ended this exercise feeling worried, but she did have a "To Do" list.

In the seminar for teachers of writing-intensive courses that I lead, teachers often raise the question of how much help they can be expected to give these student writers who are not on track, referring to such help as "coddling." Some teachers have suggested that students who can't find a focus, formulate a plan, or participate in collaboration should be left alone to suffer the natural consequences of their inadequacy. Why not just let them fail? On the other hand, I suggest, why not help them succeed?

The affective responses of this study indicate an important way in which self-assessment in the middle differs from traditional self-assessment of a finished product. Although a tacit goal of traditional self-assessment is to encourage the writer to value his or her own writing and appreciate its quality, a student assessing his or her project in the middle is engaged in a more hard-nosed, goal-oriented task. And rather than "feeling its quality" (Miller, 1982) the writer may be feeling its chaos. The writer's feelings at this point in the composing process are more likely to be negative than positive, critical than affirming, because, in fact, researching and writing a major project in the disciplines is difficult. Such assignments are designed to be intellectually challenging and to push students' learning and writing emphatically toward disciplinary competence and professional excellence. In capstone projects, self-assessment is less about giving birth to a deep expression of the self and gazing fondly into its newborn eyes; it is more about locating and coming to terms with knowledge in one's field, synthesizing, organizing, and making meaning of one's own.

Benefits and Limitations for Teachers

Although benefits accruing to students from midproject self-assessment are plentiful, teachers may have mixed responses to the exercise. Here I identify problems my colleagues and I have encountered and suggest ways in which teachers nevertheless benefit from students' freewriting in the middle.

The first problem is that the exercise takes 15 minutes of class time. Sounds quick and easy, say most teachers of writing. However, when the exercise was presented to a seminar of faculty preparing to teach writing-intensive courses in the disciplines, their eyes narrowed as they braced to resist giving up class lecture time to help students do what many believe students should do independently. Isn't this just babying them? In responding I share Berthoff's (1981) admonition: When teaching people to write, "begin with where they are" (p. 9). If students are emotionally overwhelmed by a writing project, feuding within their team, struggling with time management, or floundering for lack of focus, closing our eyes to the problems does not make them disappear. Nor can we lecture problems away. So a teacher can choose to deposit 15 minutes' worth of course content in the students' notebooks, or facilitate 15 minutes of students assessing their own writing processes, imagining solutions to their own problems, and taking responsibility for the work ahead.

The exercise not only takes valuable lecture time, it may also surface complaints about the course, the assignment, and the teacher. What should a teacher do with the resistance or criticism that may surface? If one student complains that the assignment is vague or boring or useless, then the teacher can probably assume the problem lies with the student. If a number of students cite the assignment as the major problem, the teacher would probably want to look closely at ways in which the assignment (or how it was communicated to students) could be improved.

Teacher reactions to criticism of the assignment may vary across the disciplines. Although teachers within English departments who have been trained to teach writing may be more used to student feedback on ways to improve writing assignments, reactions are more complicated for teachers of writing-intensive courses in other disciplines. As Director of the Writing Intensive Curriculum at a research university, I work with faculty from across the university who are teaching writing-intensive courses to their majors. I have come to admire the courage with which these professors take on the challenge of teaching writing. At the same time I am aware that, in spite of faculty development seminars and support from my office and from other teachers of writing, their sense of competence for the task can be somewhat fragile. Most of these engineers, chemists, geologists, and philosophers are clearly committed to helping their majors become more competent writers; some are even passionate about it. However, they may not be prepared for the sort of critiques that can surface when students do self-assessment.

Nevertheless, critiques can be useful and can teach us to become better teachers of writing. Again, the risk exists alongside the gain.

A final risk is that in student responses teachers may encounter uncomfortable truths about students' lives. For example, this "To do" list: "(a) find [materials]; (b) stop drinking; (c) go to [computer lab]; (d) fix and spell check; (e) Stop partying; (f) HIDE from friends; (g) print; (h) don't be too hung over, (i) don't think about graduation; (j) don't drink Monday night." A teacher may not *want* to wonder if a student's self-rhetoric will keep her sober until the project is due, or if her teammates will act as enablers and cover for her. A teacher may especially not want to consider whether this "To Do" list is a call for help. Freewriting in the middle can force us to consider the question of appropriate professorial distance from students' personal problems.

If becoming aware of students' affective struggles can make teachers uncomfortable, it can also improve teaching and learning in an area seldom addressed by college curricula. Freewriting in the middle is a form of affective education, engendering and encouraging a number of components identified as promoting emotional health: self-awareness, personal decision making, managing feelings, handling stress, communication, insight, self-acceptance, personal responsibility, group dynamics, and conflict resolution (Stone & Dillehunt, cited in Goleman, 1995, p. 304). Goleman, author of *Emotional Intelligence*, advocated including "emotional literacy" as part of education. Although his discussion focuses primarily on precollege education, his observations also would also seem to apply to students in higher education. According to Goleman, studies indicate that educating for emotional literacy, "improve[s students'] *academic* achievement scores and school performance" (p. 284; italics his). Goleman argued:

> In a time when too many [students] lack the capacity to handle their upsets, to listen or focus, to rein in impulse, to feel responsible for their work or care about learning, anything that will buttress these skills will help in their education. In this sense, emotional literacy enhances schools' ability to teach. (p. 284)

Freewriting in the middle also enhances teaching by inviting teachers to become what Schön (1983) called "reflective practitioners." Student responses to the exercise generate a snapshot of where individuals are at a particular moment in the major project, a snapshot in which the teacher can see who is smiling, who is angry, who is nearly in tears, which group is not speaking. The problems identified and solutions suggested can signal areas where students need more writing instruction or guidance from the teacher. Feedback can also be used to revise the assignment before it is used again. Freewriting in the middle even reduces teacher work load because most students make headway on solving their biggest writing problem *without the teacher having done anything except invest 15 minutes of class time and ask five questions.*

An example of how a teacher can benefit from reflection on student responses is seen in the experience of the Animal Science professor who participated in the study. He reported that the complaints about the assignment which surfaced through the exercise (voiced by one third of the students, a significant number) made him aware that he needed to improve his own communication of the purpose of the assignment and do a better job of helping students recognize the advantages of a real-world writing task that could actually be published. By becoming a reflective practitioner who faced students' complaints with courage and concern for effective teaching, this professor gained insight into what makes a good assignment and began planning how to revise his assignment for next year.

Cognitive problems identified by students can also remind the reflective teacher of areas of instruction needed to prepare students for major writing projects. For example, responses in this study suggest that teachers across the curriculum need to find better ways of teaching students to evaluate research material found during the search process. As a reference librarian observed after working with a writing-intensive class using the internet, students often assign equal value to a United Nations document on world hunger as they do to the personal opinions of an unidentifiable hothead on a bulletin board. Similarly, when a student's CD-rom search reveals 200 journal articles on his topic, how does he decide where to start, what to use?

The usefulness of this exercise extends to helping teachers with their own problematic writing projects. One award-winning fiction writer reported that doing the exercise helped her solve a problem in a story that had stymied her for weeks. A biologist who had just won a quarter-million-dollar grant said the 15 minutes he spent on the exercise was the first time in 6 months he had taken time to focus on the research he cares about most. Once in a late-night phone conversation I talked a despondent dissertation writer through the exercise long distance. Finishing her "To Do" list, she said, "I can do this. Thank you," and hung up.

Ideally, freewriting in the middle can become part of a writer's habitual writing strategies. Problem solving, said Stephen Covey (1989), author of *The Seven Habits of Highly Successful People,* starts with the self, with paying attention, making conscious choices, identifying options, and choosing a plan of action. And a habit, said Covey, is the intersection of knowledge (what to, why to), skills (how to), and desire (want to). Freewriting in the middle is a strategy that promotes being proactive and opens writers to the knowledge, skills, and desire to make a habit of solving their own writing problems. It can help transform the daunting middle of writing from messy muddle to mindful movement as students across the curriculum become effective problem solvers and successful writers.

REFERENCES

Bandura, A. (1976). Self-reinforcement: Theoretical and methodological considerations. *Behaviorism, 4*, 135-155.

Bandura, A. (1977a). Self-efficacy: Toward a unifying theory of behavioral change. *Psychological Review, 84*, 191-215.

Bandura, A. (1977). *Social learning theory.* Englewood Cliffs, NJ: Prentice-Hall.

Berthoff, A. E. (1981). *The making of meaning.* Upper Montclair, NJ: Boynton Cook.

Bolles, R. C. (1972). Reinforcement, expectancy, and learning. *Psychological Review, 79*, 394-409.

Covey, S. (1989). *The seven habits of highly successful people.* New York: Simon and Schuster.

Elbow, P. (1981). *Writing without teachers.* New York: Oxford University Press.

Elbow, P., & Belanoff, P. (1989). *A community of writers.* New York: McGraw-Hill.

Flower, L. (1981). *Problem-solving strategies for writing.* New York: Harcourt, Brace Jovanovich.

Flower, L. S., & Hayes, J. R. (1981, December). A cognitive process theory of writing. *College Composition and Communication, 32*, 365-387.

Goleman, D. (1995). *Emotional intelligence.* New York: Bantam.

Macrorie, K. (1968). *Writing to be read.* Rochelle Park, NJ: Hayden.

Miller, S. (1982, May). How writers evaluate their own writing. *College Composition and Communication, 33*, 176-183.

Schön, D. A. (1983). *The reflective practitioner: How professionals think in action.* New York: Basic Books.

8 "KNOW YOUR KNOWLEDGE": JOURNALS AND SELF-ASSESSMENT

Jane Bowman Smith

Winthrop University

Self-assessment has a dual nature, and for many teachers and researchers, the term itself is almost an oxymoron. Self-assessment is a reflective *and* an evaluative act, both personal *and* public—and if my students are representative, it is not something they have to do often in their academic classrooms. Students who are asked to do self-assessments are often confused or wary: Despite my careful explanation, they cannot fully understand my purposes for having them first think about what they have learned and then evaluate their own work. They believe that such evaluation is the teacher's responsibility.

Self-assessment is not evaluation in the sense of assigning a grade, but students often assume this is what they are being asked to do. Perhaps their education has trained them; teacher response often takes the form of grading only. Yet students need to be given the opportunity, as Berthoff (1982) said, to know their own knowing: "To know your knowledge is to search for meanings, to discover and articulate relationships" (p. 234). But how does one "know one's knowledge"? Students find it difficult to think about something this abstract. Yet such activity has been found to be essential to a real education. The work of cognitive psychologists—and particularly that of Bruner—suggests, as does Berthoff, that one must think about one's learning before one truly learns. Cognitive psychology offers a rationale for claiming the *necessity* of student self-assessment in our classrooms.

This chapter, therefore, has two sections: In the first, I briefly review the cognitive argument for self-assessment, and then discuss certain relevant aspects of the teacher/student relationship that may affect the use of self-assessment techniques. In the second, I discuss some of my own students' commentaries to suggest the range of student response and the sorts of information self-assessments can provide not only to the students themselves, but to their teachers.

Self-assessment as a technique is firmly rooted in theories of learning. Bruner (1964) claimed:

> Learning . . . is to climb on your own shoulders to be able to look down on what you have just done and then to represent it to yourself. Manipulation and representation, then, in continuing cycles are necessary conditions for discovery. They are the antithesis of passive, listener like learning. Yet representation is not frenzied activity. Though active, it is still ratiocination, a going back over experience, a listening to oneself. (p. 101)

Perry (1970) posited that the essential difference between the intellectual and the anti-intellectual is the habit of metacognition:

> We have come to believe from all these hours of listening that the anti-intellectual, be he in or out of college, is definable not as "against thinking," but against thinking about one particular thing: thought. Most particularly his *own* thought.
>
> In contrast, the liberally educated man, be he a graduate of college or not, is one who has learned to think about his own thoughts, to examine the way he orders his data and the assumptions he is making, and to compare these with other thoughts that other men might have. . . . From this position, he can take responsibility for his own stand and negotiate—with respect—with other men. (pp. 39-40)

The implication of Perry's statement is that we do not all learn to think about our thinking. Bruner (1986) suggested that the culture in which we live can encourage (or presumably discourage) our metacognitive activity. He argued:

> An *Anlage* of metacognition is present as early as the eighteenth month of life. How much and in what form it develops will, it seems reasonable to suppose, depend upon the demands of the culture in which one lives—represented by particular others one encounters and by some notion of a "generalized other" that one forms. (p. 67)

It is surely the teacher's responsibility, as one of the most important of the "particular others" who represent culture, to enable the child to engage in this meaning-making activity. "How much and in what form" we encourage the student to develop this ability is a key question, not only of this chapter, but of this volume.

Bruner (1964) suggested that teachers need to learn to teach their students "to listen to what they have been doing so that their actions can be converted into representations of what they have done and what has resulted" (p. 101). Berthoff (1990) would agree; she asserted that students need time to "interpret their interpretations," and thus to learn that they have, in fact, learned:

> Students do not need to learn to interpret nor do they need to learn how to interpret their interpretations: they are born interpreters. But they must discover *that* this is so. We should offer them assisted invitations to discover *what* they are doing and thereby *how* to do it. Relating the that, the what, and the how, each to the others, is a dialectical, recursive, critical, and creative process which spirals on toward a pedagogy of knowing. (p. 59)

Berthoff suggests a critical problem here. Our learning is often tacit; we don't know consciously that we are learning from our own actions, our trials and errors. As teachers, we need to help our students make this process both *conscious* and *purposive*. Self-assessment techniques thus offer two valuable contributions to student learning: They allow for what both Bruner and Perry see as essential, time for reflection—and the opportunity to create for oneself what Berthoff sees as the foundation for future knowledge.

The effective teacher's goal, then, should be to set up the classroom so that learning becomes cyclical: Students act and learn, reflect on their actions, and then verbalize their learning in order to realize it—which leads to new action and new learning. Ultimately, students must learn to examine not only the products of their learning, but their own thinking processes, to engage in metacognitive activity. The teacher's challenge is to help the student establish this habit of metacognition by providing a means, perhaps through heuristics or a more open form of response, and then by encouraging the student to share the results with others when appropriate.

The written commentaries that students produce as a result of self-assessment provide valuable insights into student learning. The practical benefit to the teacher is simply explained: Student self-assessments provide information that improves instruction by allowing teachers to respond directly to the problems students identify. However, there are other benefits as well. The self-assessments create a dialogue between teacher and student and a better chance for mutual learning. The students' benefits from self-assessment are perhaps more important, however. First, the procedure urges them to examine their work and their thinking carefully and ponder its meaning; second, as a result of this reflection, they become more aware of what they have learned; finally, they assign a value both to the work itself and to the learning it represents. All three phases of this process are essential: learning, knowing *that* you have learned, and knowing *what* you have learned.

Assigning self-assessment in the classroom, despite its obvious value to both teacher and students, does have potential dangers. Self-assessment can easily (although unintentionally) be used to serve the teacher's ends and not the students'. As Brookfield (1995) warned, "One of the hardest things teachers have to learn is that the sincerity of their intentions does not guarantee the purity of their practice" (p. 1). Teachers can "take over" the process by looking for one right answer or even a particular kind of response. They can also take over the student's text through extensive commentary that may too narrowly define future learning or experimentation. We can also inadvertently become oppressive, Brookfield argued, by insisting that students reveal their ignorance or problems they have had without first establishing a climate of trust in our classrooms.

Brookfield (1995) also warned us against "teaching innocently," (p. 1) of assuming that students understand our motives and purposes in the same way that we ourselves do. We have to understand both our own and our students' places in the classroom hierarchy and the effect that this relationship has on the students' responses to us. The fact that the teacher reads these self-assessments affects what students will write, and this effect is both positive and negative. The positive is that students will see that we value this work, and thus perhaps take it more seriously. Their greater commitment then leads to greater learning. The negative is that the fact of our reading may change what the student writes in ways that are not beneficial to the student. The teacher's goal should not be to engender some "correct" answer, or even a general type of response, but rather to encourage the process itself.

In assigning self-assessment, we must be sensitive to our students' possible perception both of us as teachers and the assignment itself. Brookfield (1995) argued that "students' awareness of the power relationship that exists between themselves and their teachers is such that it pervades nearly all interactions between them" (p. 11). Often, the self-assessments show only what the students are willing to reveal; the responses may also suggest what they *think* the teacher wants them to reveal. We must be aware, then, when using our students' comments for our own information that these responses are situated within a hierarchy—the classroom—and may show signs of the "chameleon effect": At best, the students' commentaries will reflect what has gone on in the classroom—the goals, values, instructional methods, and actual content—but also the students' desire to say what they think we want to hear. In a sense, this is the paradox of teaching: We want students to be honestly converted. We do not want them *cynically* to write down our own words and toss them back at us.

Most importantly, however, Brookfield(1995) warned that "we may easily overestimate students' willingness and ability to reflect on how and what they are learning" (p. 97). We thus have to reevaluate our purposes in having them self-assess. Our goal need not be for them to recreate our evaluation of their work; "mini-teaching" is not the point. Their examination and learning from their own learning—in their own way—is what is important. And we should remember that a student's learning often runs ahead of what she is able to verbalize. In order to improve the chances for student learning, we must remember to contextualize these (and other) assignments so that students understand as much as is possible about our purposes.

The self-assessments I discuss were written in a sophomore-level survey of World Literature—a "great works" course. In general, the enrollment is a minimum of 35 students, and most are not English majors. For many, this is a required course. These students struggle with the reading, typically 20 pages of an anthology per class; they also struggle with their own lack of historical background, their sometimes weak writing, and their lack of confidence in their ability to interpret literature. The students' primary writing assignment is a reading-response journal. The journal fulfills a practical teaching purpose because the students read more carefully, think about the literature before they write, and thus come to class better prepared. Yet as has been discussed by others (for example, see Fulweiler, 1987), the journal also aids students in their understanding and interpreting of literature and is itself a reflective assignment that urges the students to focus on their own responses. The students are required to write one page (250 words) about the assigned reading for each class period—usually twice a week. I collect their entries before the beginning of each class in part to prevent students from using class discussion as the basis of their journal entries. The students receive a handout that explains their options for writing: to explore their feelings about the work, to discuss characterization, theme, language, and so forth, or to compare the work to something else they have read. Students are also urged to write speculatively, to identify problems that they have with the literature, and to ask questions. I do not read or respond to every entry a student writes; I encourage them to see the journal as their own creative work.

The students evaluate the work they have done in their journals at midterm—to allow for goal setting—and again at the end of the term. These two separate self-assessments are "endpoint" assignments, intended to help the students see their journals as something more than a collection of separate, unconnected pieces. Students often compartmentalize their learning; they often see each entry as a separate response and reach intellectual closure with each piece of writing. The act of self-assessment urges the students to see the *wholeness* of their journals as well as that each journal is greater than the sum of its parts. Ideally, they realize in the act of self-assessing that the journal has become an ongoing narrative of their learning. In a sense, these self-assessments show the students at a threshold of learning: They are often assessing their work themselves for the first time, and they tend to react to the assignment in predictable ways.

The actual self-assessment procedure is simple. I distribute questions, and the students' responses serve as journal entries. These are typical midterm questions:

1. How would you evaluate your writing at this point? What are your strengths? Did you have any problems I can help you with?
2. Describe what you see in your journal writing. What kinds of responses to the literature have you experimented with?
3. In what ways do you hope to improve your journal over the rest of the term?

The questions at the end of the term are similar:

1. Describe the kinds of writing you did in your journal at the beginning of the term; then, describe the kinds of writing you did at the end (it might help to look at the subject matter, whether you were recording facts, discussing your personal reactions, etc.). What changes do you notice, if any? Why do you think these changes (if any) occurred? If none did, why not?
2. What do you feel you did well in your journal? What would you have liked to improve?
3. Do you feel that keeping a journal in this class was worthwhile? Why or why not? If you felt that this was a worthwhile experience, what particular value(s) did the journal have for you?
4. Is there anything that could be done to make the journal assignment more effective and useful for the students?

Students often write at midterm that being asked to read over and analyze their work comes as a surprise; in the past, they tell me, they usually did the assignments, read a teacher's comments, and then filed their work away. The process of seeing their work as a whole, of making connections among the entries, of seeing trends in their thought, is energizing. And when they *do* examine their entries critically, they realize what they have accomplished. Describing what they had done in midterm question #2 leads them naturally to setting goals in #3. Even simple goals like "I need to work more on understanding characterization" provides some focus for learning.

Not only is the act of self-assessment important to the student and his or her learning, the commentaries also provide valuable information to the teacher. In their self-assessment commentaries, these students tend to report that there are three major benefits to keeping a journal: (a) practical uses related to studying, (b) a means to engage in dialogue with the instructor, and (c) a means both to demonstrate and to further their learning. In spite of the work that is involved, most students are positive about having to keep a journal; once they realize the practical benefits to their work, only a very few complain, and usually this is due to the "lack of time to do a good job." Obviously, this comment can be seen as teacher-based: What better reason could they present to an English teacher?!

The self-assessments reveal that many students tend to be very practical; despite the reflective, personal nature of the writing (which I try to foster with my comments), they tend to define the journal as a study aid. This serves as an often-needed reminder that not all my students value literature and writing in the ways that I do. The journal assignment provides discipline for some, because they admit that they keep up with the reading to write their entries; many use it to formulate questions for class discussion; many find it useful to help prepare for tests. In reading their commentaries, however, it becomes clear that students do make a connection between writing and memory, as Jennifer's response suggested:

> It is definitely true that you remember something when you write it down. The journal made it easy when you came to tests to make a chart with characters' names, authors, titles, and a quick summary.

Jennifer's journal entries thus serve as a convenient summary of the literary work—and, in a second writing activity, she distills her journal entries, preparing a study guide. Her writing had become a record of her knowledge. Other students, however, discover, as they evaluate their journals, that the original act of writing has established a context for memory, as did Anne:

> Having the journal let me reread my entries before the test and as I
> did it, I remembered writing it and the way I felt about the work.
> The story would all come back in a rush.

Rereading the entry recalled to Anne her act of writing: Not only does
the emotional context return—"the way I felt about the work"—but the
story itself "comes back in a rush." Emig (1978) has suggested that as
many writers compose, "the action of the hand, the literal act of writing,
the motoric component" may be "crucial," and she proposed that the
physical act of writing "may reinforce in some way the work of the left
hemisphere of the brain" (p. 60-61). Significantly, Anne wrote that as she
read, she remembered the *act* of writing the journal—and this "physical
memory" brought the story back to her. For some students, then, the
physical component of writing serves two functions: Not only does it
further the original act of thinking, but remembering the physical act of
writing allows them to tap into their original sense of discovery.

The self-assessments reveal that the second major value of the
journal for some students is its providing a means of engaging in
dialogue with me—the teacher—without the "interference" imposed by
the class at large. Some students' responses, like Tricia's, suggested that
they needed more time to reflect than that allowed in the "rough and
tumble" of class discussion:

> The journal allowed me to discuss my likes and dislikes of certain
> stories without putting myself on the spot and mixing up my
> thoughts because of my dislike for speaking up in class. Another
> plus was asking questions and getting one-on-one feedback from
> you. It helped to make the class more personal which is rare in
> classes as large as ours with limited time. It also allows one to
> express herself if she chooses to in ways that she may not be able to
> in class—or even on a more private, face-to-face teacher-student
> basis.

Note Tricia's anxiety over "mixing up her thoughts" and her need for
learning to be made "personal," which Bruner (1964) argued is essential.
The journal, then, can become for introspective students a means of
individualizing their learning; it can allow both student and teacher to
address the issues that concern the student. Tricia has learned, as Probst
(1989) suggested, that teachers can be "individuals, representing a
culture and a discipline, with whom to talk" (p. 77). The "talk" does not
need to be verbal; and as we all know, in a class of 35 students, too often
a few tend to dominate class discussion. It is easy to assume that the
silent students are not fully participating. A quiet student's self-
assessment can serve to remind the teacher that sometimes students

who resist participation may have reasons for their silence other than lack of preparedness or laziness.

Perhaps the most important information provided by the students' self-assessments concerns their examination of the journal as a record of their learning, and descriptions of the growth in their reading, writing, and critical-thinking skills. This smaller group of students is perhaps most aware of changes in their writing ability over the course of the semester. Regular practice allows them to gain confidence both from their own belief in their writing's success and my comments on their journals. The changes they notice are often modeled on class goals; they use my comments as well as class discussion to form their criteria, which suggests how contextualized self-assessments are. Many, for example, saw a shift from general to much more specific writing, which was one of the course goals. "In the beginning of the course," Brenda wrote,

> my journal responses were very general. I would say, "I liked this reading" without giving any reasons why. Then I began saying why I liked an assignment, but I gave very general reasons. Eventually, I became specific; if I liked a reading, I gave specific reasons why and if I disliked a reading I gave particular reasons for that too.

Brenda's self-assessment suggests that practice—and teacherly admonitions—can actually produce results that students *see*. Brenda has learned that her opinions need to be supported with "specific reasons," not just asserted.

Students also report that they develop fluency. The self-assessment makes them aware that they have created a more comfortable connection between thinking and writing, of using their writing as a means to think more deeply. Some state, as did Sam, that they gradually become both more comfortable and more confident with writing:

> My responses became much longer. They didn't seem forced any more while at the beginning of the semester, I actually had to sit there for an hour to think of things to say. Rarely were my responses over three-fourths of a page because of this forced writing.

Sam pointed out something valuable here: Over the course of the semester, the writing practice alleviated his discomfort and thus his reticence. In confronting the white page class after class, students begin to develop their own strategies for filling it up with writing; they experiment and take risks. "Forced writing" becomes more natural. Sam gave further evidence of increased fluency later, when he wrote, "From the play *The Lion and the Jewel*, I picked out one particular line and wrote a whole page on it. This is just one example of my success." Sam's self-assessment demonstrates that he realized he had learned how to interpret; he had seen for himself that he discussed one line for an entire page. The procedure has allowed him to define "success" for himself, to recognize his achievement for himself.

The self-assessment commentaries also offer insight into how students use their writing to respond to literature. Summarizing the text is a very common student response to difficult literature. Jim's commentary is typical of students who began the semester summarizing what they read. Yet he (and others) suggested that summarizing is not necessarily laziness on the student's part:

> My journals at the beginning of the term were short. But they were to the point. I was mostly writing about how I didn't understand or how confused I was after reading the stories. My writings were more or less just brief summaries of the stories and my opinion. Near the end of the term, my writings changed. I started asking myself more questions about the stories. I even started answering them with why I thought something happened. I also started writing some longer journals that really made some sense. I feel that these changes occurred because I really wanted to get something out of these stories. I was also spending more time thinking about what I wanted to write. I took more time in writing them, too.

Jim's response suggests that his early difficulties with his journal writing stemmed from confusion and a lack of confidence in his own ability to interpret literature; a summary allowed him to write something he was sure of. Yet he apparently was able to profit from class discussion—he began to ask himself questions—modeling his journal responses after the normal class procedures. He developed fluency, now "spending more time thinking" about the literature and used the act of writing to bring forth ideas. In his commentary, Jim charted his own growth, suggesting that he had begun to learn how to read and understand literature for himself. His question-and-answer format empowered him; he had seen that he did not need to rely on the teacher for answers—or, indeed, for the questions. What began as teacher-centered journal entries became for him student-centered responses. It is not surprising that Jim put this knowledge into "teacher-centered" terms; later in this entry he wrote, "I knew more what was expected." However, the skills he has developed are still his own. He has learned, and knows he has learned, a technique that will become the basis for future learning.

One of the goals of any sophomore survey is to help students learn to interpret literature. The language they use—"tear up the story, rip it apart," and the "hidden meaning"—all suggest that they see the act of interpretation as destructive. "Hidden" is particularly significant: Only the teacher, they believe, possesses secret knowledge of what the story or poem means.

Interpretation begins with the reading of the text, and self-assessments suggest that writing journal entries changes the way some students read. Some specifically claim that knowing they have to write a journal makes them more attentive; they mark their texts, engaging in a "writing to learn" approach. Michelle's response is typical of these students:

> At first, I hated the idea of writing a journal. But, I can say now that it was definitely worthwhile. I knew I had to write a journal entry, so I underlined things as I read. I paid more attention to detail. I read more carefully and looked for things that were hidden in the story. Writing a journal has helped me to read more comparatively. As I read something, I compare the work or a character in the work to others. Writing a journal has also helped me to learn to use quotations from a work to get particular points across.

Although Michelle saw the meaning as "hidden," she has engaged the text through reading and then writing. Her language reveals her confidence; she has learned how to use evidence to get her "particular points across." Michelle's self-assessment demonstrates, with its discussion of her underlining and searching out of detail, that she was doing the groundwork for literary interpretation, and that the imposed discipline of the journal pays off for students.

However, not all the information is positive. The self-assessments sometimes reveal painful blocking, reticence, or self-censoring in students' thinking. Beth saw little change in her ability to interpret literature:

> I didn't note any big changes; most of my journal is recorded facts. Facts are safe. I have a hard time trying to tell what I feel is important. Example: we are shown an ink blot and are asked to write what we see. The other students write down animals—birds, dogs, cows—and other shapes. I write down "an ink blot."

Beth's commentary suggests two related problems. Perhaps she feared a possible negative response to her ideas, and so apparently suppressed them ("Facts are safe"). She also seemed to believe that she had no imagination, no ability to interpret language imaginatively, and thus clung to the literal. She was apparently unaware that her writing is superior to that of many other students; Michelle, quoted earlier, revealed more confidence, and yet Beth's writing displays syntactic variation, short sentences for emphasis, and dramatic presentation—her control of her own writing is impressive. Ironically, her use of an analogy here—interpreting literature is like seeing things in an inkblot—suggests that she *is* capable of imaginative thinking. Beth's commentary, as sad as it is, is valuable; her response reveals the frustration of students who fear the particular demands of our courses. And she had at least identified and explored her problem for herself.

Other students also realize self-imposed limits at the end of the term through the self-assessment process, as Kirk, for example, did:

> Maybe students should be required to use only their feelings in the journal. If summaries were ruled out, maybe I could have found the significance of the story. Summarizing a story does not really make a person think about the meaning. Interpretation is a better way to use the journal.

Although Kirk was still relying on the teacher for guidance in his wish that there had been a "rule" to force him to take a specific approach, the self-assessment had allowed him to make this discovery about interpretation for himself. And Kirk has made a cognitive "leap": He has realized that he has only been summarizing; he has begun to define the act of interpretation for himself. His entry, however, gave me information that allowed me to clarify how one interprets literature in class; others were also confused about the role of one's feelings in a good response and saw "their feelings" as synonymous with "interpretation." Kirk's entry shows that he understood that there is something beyond the literal words on the page, something that should be expressed in his own words, even though he, like Michelle, referred to the meaning as something "hidden" in the story.

What is most satisfying in reading these commentaries, however, is realizing that some students do see the underlying purpose of the journal as a means to help them create their own knowledge. Rick, who was planning to teach, was particularly interested in the journal as a tool of exploration:

> The journals provided us with a unique opportunity to evaluate and explore each work, using our own thoughts and interpretations. This means so much more than just "memorizing" lecture notes and regurgitating it on the test. When people aren't allowed to think analytically for themselves, I don't think they recall anything they study. Students can't read, evaluate, and write about a work without forming an opinion of it and learning something in the process.

As Rick wrote, he shifted from his own use of the journal as a means to learn to speculating about students in general. Rick's contrasting of "memorizing lecture notes" with "[thinking] analytically for themselves" suggested that Rick had made this knowledge his own. Further, this commentary makes it clear to me that Rick no longer believed that there is only one right answer, namely, the teacher's; and this insight will inform his own teaching.

Finally, many students experienced a surprised pride in themselves as a result of the self-assessment process, as did Marty:

> I was amazed at the way I could express myself. I really feel that towards the end of my journal it got better because I could just get into it and write, write, write. I know that when I was writing, new things would just constantly pop into my head. I just didn't think I'd have enough paper to write on sometimes.

That "amazed" reveals Marty's pride in her achievement and in what she learned. In contemplating her work, she remembered her growth: By the end of the semester, she knew that the act of writing engendered "constant" thought.

It should by now have become clear that the process of self-assessment is useful both to the teacher and to the students. In reading these responses, a teacher learns valuable practical information: I can see, for example, what the students learn in keeping a journal; I can improve the assignment and my responses to future students, based on what these students have said. It is easier to justify the journal to subsequent classes by discussing past students' comments on what they found useful. However, self-assessments are also valuable to me because I benefit from the students' insights into their processes of learning. Reading about the students' struggles and successes with both interpretation of and writing about literature has made me a more sensitive teacher.

Self-assessment, however, is important primarily to the students themselves, as an essential part of their learning, a critical step in the act of knowing. Students need to be given time to reflect on their work and their thinking, to realize what they have learned, and to use this learning as a foundation for later learning. Strategies that help students to practice this process are a midway point between dependence on the teacher's evaluation and their eventual independence as critical thinkers. Berthoff (1990) claimed that "it is by interpreting our interpretations that we make the meanings which will serve as the means for making further meaning" (p. 59). In doing these self-assessments, the students recognize and identify what they have learned, thus making it more fully their own.

REFERENCES

Berthoff, A. E. (1982). *Forming thinking writing: The composing imagination.* Montclair, NJ: Boynton/Cook.

Berthoff, A. E. (1990). *The sense of learning.* Portsmouth, NH: Boynton/Cook.

Brookfield, S. D. (1995). *Becoming a critically reflective teacher.* San Francisco: Jossey-Bass.

Bruner, J. S. (1964). *On knowing: Essays for the left hand.* Cambridge, MA: Harvard University Press.

Bruner, J. S. (1986). *Actual minds, possible worlds.* Cambridge, MA: Harvard University Press.

Emig, J. (1978). Hand, eye, brain: Some basics in the composing process. In C. R. Cooper & L. Odell (Eds.), *Research on composing: Points of departure* (pp. 59-83). Urbana, IL: National Council of Teachers of English.

Fulweiler, T. (Ed.). (1987). *The journal book.* Portsmouth, NH: Boynton/Cook.

Perry, W. G. (1970). *Forms of intellectual and ethical development in the college years.* New York: Holt, Rinehart & Winston.

Probst, R. E. (1989). Transactional theory and response to student writing. In C. M. Anson (Ed.), *Writing and response: Theory, practice, and research* (pp. 68-79). Urbana, IL: National Council of Teachers of English.

9 SELF-ASSESSMENT, REFLECTION, AND THE NEW TEACHER OF WRITING

Irwin Weiser

Purdue University

As Yancey (1994) pointed out, graduate teaching assistants in composition programs "often come to their teaching 'underprepared'" (p. 211). She explained that at many large universities, new teaching assistants assigned to composition courses frequently have taken no teacher-preparation, rhetoric, or other courses that might provide them with some theoretical and practical background for the responsibilities they are to face. She also reminded us that "some of them will not want to teach writing at all; they won't bring the enthusiasm and commitment we'd like to see in all colleagues" (p. 211). This should not surprise us, because the majority of graduate students in English have come to study literature, theory, or creative writing, not rhetoric and composition, and they envision their careers to be centered around scholarship, writing, and teaching in those areas. As I have noted elsewhere, (Weiser, 1990), very often graduate students in English studies have not themselves even taken undergraduate composition courses: Their interests and abilities in language, reading, and writing have frequently allowed them to test or place out of introductory composition courses. Nevertheless, new graduate students are often expected to assume full responsibility for teaching first-year composition courses after only a few days of orientation and preparation, and with most of their support and instruction coming in the form of an in-service practicum or seminar. Such approaches can, I believe, be not only supportive and helpful to the instructors, but also effective means of introducing them to teaching. All too often, however, these preterm orientations and in-service courses are so intensive and so practice-and problem-oriented that they leave little opportunity for the teaching assistants to reflect on their pedagogical practices and the various subject positions they assume as teachers.

In this chapter, I discuss several strategies to encourage graduate students new to teaching to become, in Schön's (1987) now familiar phrase, "reflective practitioners," capable of reflecting on, reviewing, evaluating, and revising their teaching practices. In doing so, I necessarily also suggest how writing program administrators and faculty mentors can facilitate collaborative, supportive, and nonthreatening self-assessment.

The specific strategies I discuss include a preservice survey sent to all new teaching assistants prior to their arrival at Purdue, a midsemester self- and course evaluation I have recently begun using with teaching assistants in the practicum in teaching college composition I teach, the selection of end-of-the-semester student-evaluation questions, and teaching portfolios, which are quickly becoming a widely used approach to teacher development, reflection, and evaluation. The first three of these strategies and the instruments that have been developed to implement them are components of the composition program at Purdue, while teaching portfolios have become part of teacher preparation and development in schools, college, and universities across the country.

THE PRESERVICE SURVEY AND REFLECTIVE PRACTICE

It may seem odd to consider a preservice survey as a method of encouraging reflective practice, but for reasons that become clear later, I believe that by asking new teachers to think about what their roles will be before they assume those roles, we begin a process of consciousness raising about teaching in general and teaching composition specifically. The survey, reproduced in its entirety in Appendix A, elicits several kinds of information about the respondents' prior educational and teaching experience and then asks them to rank, according to their interest in discussing and learning about them, four groups of items concerning teaching. What those of us who plan the orientation program and practicum learn from the responses helps us reflect ourselves on the practices we will need to address. For instance, knowing that, as was the case a few years ago, nearly half of the new teaching assistants had not taught at all and 79% of them had not taught composition enabled us to decide that we needed to emphasize general matters concerning teaching, such as establishing course policies, dealing with student problems, and planning and carrying out classroom discussions in addition to focusing on the specifics of teaching writing. However, this year we learned that nearly 75% of the new teaching assistants had taught composition elsewhere. We organized our practicum sections so that the inexperienced teachers worked together and received help in both general teaching and specific composition strategies, whereas the experienced instructors spent more time discussing the approaches they would be using in our program and reflecting on how those approaches differed from and were similar to their previous experiences.

The second section of the survey, the ranking of four groups of items concerning teaching, complements and extends the general information we receive from the responses to items in the first section. Many of the items are intended to encourage new teachers to reflect on their responsibilities as a teacher (items in Group 1) or their status as graduate teaching assistants (the first two items in Group 4), whereas others, particularly those in Groups 2 and 3, are more directly focused on what it means to teach writing. The very existence of items on the list can inform instructors about what our program values and can thus prepare them for a course in which, for example, students are encouraged to consider the audience for whom they write and are expected to work collaboratively with one another. Experienced teachers entering our program may find that the questions we ask in Group 3 allow them to reflect on how their work here will build on their previous teaching whereas inexperienced teachers will begin to think about teaching and writing in the terms of the process orientation of our program. As Director of Composition, I have been able to consider how each year's new group of teaching assistants can be introduced to our program, and along with the faculty mentors, can revise the orientation and practicum based on some insight into who the participants will be. Thus this preservice survey not only encourages our incoming staff to reflect on pedagogical concepts and issues related to their role as instructor/student, but also provides them with the opportunity to contribute to the content and emphasis of their orientation and practicum. By responding to the survey, they are encouraged to begin a process of reflection on and assessment of themselves as teachers that continues throughout their work at Purdue, and, their responses enable the faculty who mentor them to assess and revise our own practices.

MIDSEMESTER SELF- AND COURSE EVALUATIONS

The Midsemester Self- and Course Evaluation (Appendix B) is an instrument I have recently begun to use to continue and encourage the reflective self-assessment that the preservice survey begins, both for the teaching assistants I work with and for myself as their mentor. Although not formally grouped, the questions move from three that encourage teaching assistants (in the case of those I work with, usually first-time teachers) to reflect on the act/art of teaching as they have begun to experience it, to two that ask them to assess their strengths and weaknesses as teachers, to two that focus on the course itself, and finally to two questions about the practicum. The act/art of teaching questions encourage teaching assistants to consider the complexity of what they are being asked to do, acknowledging that teaching is always—and can always be viewed as—a mixture of pleasure, surprise, and frustration. All of us as teachers understand and are familiar with the frustrations, and it is easy to allow them to overshadow the satisfaction that teaching also holds and the surprises students spring on us.

For beginning teachers—who often lack confidence in their ability to teach effectively and their knowledge of what they are teaching, who are uncertain about how to wear the new authority that their position as teacher provides them, who worry about filling the class time and grading fairly—being asked to reflect on what is positive about teaching is especially important. Typically, they write about the pleasure of interacting with students, getting to know them individually. They recognize the satisfaction of helping students see new possibilities for their papers. They are pleased when they see the connection between a class presentation or discussion and improvement in a student's writing. They are surprised, more than anything else, by the passivity of their students and by their apparent unfamiliarity with and lack of interest in social and intellectual issues. They are frustrated by students who come to class unprepared, who seem to resist learning. These reflections, prompted by the first three questions, have provided us with the opportunity to discuss a number of issues: the difficulty of teaching one of the few university-wide required courses, the accompanying negative attitudes some students have to requirements that they do not see as related to their personal educational goals, nonpunitive strategies for addressing students' lack of preparation, and the reality that, as one instructor wrote recently, "I simply am not going to reach some of these kids."

In reflecting on their strengths and weaknesses, many instructors have noted the differences between their apparent success in working with individual students in conferences and their dissatisfaction with how they conduct class discussions and presentations. Several felt that they have assumed their students would be more willing participants in discussion and have realized that they must do more to prepare to draw out and encourage students to talk with one another rather than simply responding to a teacher-asked question. They have begun to understand that often a successful class is one in which most of the instructor's work has been done prior to entering the classroom, that time they spend in planning writing and discussion activities yields the kinds of interactions and enthusiastic participation they seek.

Comments about the course have proved be more immediately helpful to me than I imagine they have been to the teaching assistants. In general, teaching assistants have been satisfied with the structure of the course and the textbook and other materials I have chosen for us. Because for most of them teaching this course has been their first exposure to composing-process pedagogy, it has been gratifying to find that teaching writing-as-process and using a portfolio grading system have been consistently listed in response to the sixth question, which asks them what aspect of the course they are most satisfied with. However, I have also learned from instructors that some would like ideas about incorporating a variety of media into the course, some would be interested in discussing how the course could be organized around specific topics or issues, and others are dissatisfied with the approach to peer review we have been using. Often, teaching assistants have commented specifically on changes they will make when they teach the course again, a clear indication that they are engaged in reflection and assessment. Additionally, their responses to these questions and to the last two on the evaluation encourage me to assess what is working and what should be revised—an especially vital part of my teaching the practicum because I rarely have the opportunity to teach a section of first-year composition myself.

SELECTING END-OF-TERM STUDENT EVALUATION QUESTIONS

Students' evaluations of their instructors are what most educators and students think of when they consider evaluating teachers. The end-of-the-term evaluation of instructors by their students has an established place in higher education, and despite whatever our personal opinions of such evaluations might be, research has shown that student evaluation is both reliable and valid, if the instrument is appropriately designed and appropriately interpreted (see Seldin, 1980, 1991; Braskamp, Brandenbury, & Ory, 1984, for summaries of research). In the paragraphs that follow, I first briefly describe the development of our present evaluation questionnaire (reproduced as Appendix C), then discuss how we have tried to make its use part of encouraging teaching assistants to reflect on their pedagogical practice.

Our evaluation questions have evolved over the past several years, prompted by the recognition of the department's composition committee that neither the university-wide cafeteria system—despite its over 200 questions from which instructors can make selections—nor the briefer, yet nevertheless generic, departmental form, was appropriate for evaluating the teaching of introductory composition. Neither form allowed instructors or anyone else looking at it to determine if students believed the goals of the writing program were being met, and neither allowed instructors to tailor the evaluation questions to reflect particular pedagogical approaches or intellectual emphases. Questions on both forms were of the type Weimer (1990) has identified as global, rather than departmental, programmatic, or individual.

The present 58-item form was devised to address these weaknesses. Its initial 38 questions, nearly equally divided between those that focus primarily on the course and those that focus on the instructor, were developed by the composition committee, which includes teaching assistants as members. In keeping with our goal of including teaching assistants in their preparation and evaluation, however, there is an open invitation for them to request the addition of new questions, and thus the questionnaire has grown by 20 items, recommended by teaching assistants subsequent to the initial introduction of the questionnaire.[1] The ability of instructors to add questions enables them to develop questionnaires that are consistent with their pedagogical practices and is one way in which the questionnaire encourages reflective practice. For instance, an instructor who teaches regularly in a computer classroom and who takes advantage of the graphic and layout features of the networked software requested that items 40 and 42 be added, whereas several others whose teaching is influenced by cultural studies suggested items 44-46.

The selection of the specific questions each teaching assistant uses is another way the evaluation form encourages reflection. Although all instructors must select the 10 items the composition committee has identified as a program core,[2] beyond those (and the five university-wide core items), instructors are free to choose from among the remaining items on the list, selecting those which they feel best represent the goals of the specific courses they are teaching. This decision-making process requires that teaching assistants consider

---

[1]Because our evaluation forms are prepared and summarized by the university's Center for Instructional Services in the same format as the more general cafeteria system, the five university core questions, items 901-905, are automatically included along with those developed by the composition staff.

[2]These program core items are numbers 1, 5, 11, 12, 20, 21, 22, 24, 30, and 32 on the list in Appendix C.

which questions are most appropriate given what they have addressed in their classes. They have to anticipate whether there are specific questions students they have taught would be unlikely to respond positively to, and in doing so, have the opportunity to reflect on whether their practices should be revised. If they do not ask students particular questions, does that mean they realize they have neglected something they should have taught, or does it mean that for the specific course, those questions are not relevant? For instance, items 14–19 are particularly appropriate for courses that focus on academic writing. An instructor whose course had a different focus, as is the case for the first course in our two-semester sequence, would be making an error in judgment to include those questions, whereas an instructor teaching our second-semester or accelerated course, both of which do include an academic focus, would be missing an opportunity to assess his or her teaching (and probably some high evaluations) by omitting them.

First-year teaching assistants and their mentors discuss the questionnaire and the implications of specific questions during a practicum meeting, thus linking the evaluation with teacher preparation and self-assessment. In addition, most mentors meet individually with teaching assistants to discuss the evaluations after the tabulated and summarized questionnaires have been returned. It has been particularly helpful to meet with teaching assistants who have been discouraged by their evaluations, because they frequently pay more attention to their own ranking on the 5-point scale than they do the relationship between their own score and the mean score for all instructors who used that item.[3] That is, they see their own "3" rating as an indication of weakness rather than as being higher or lower than the mean score. Such discussions help teaching assistants place their evaluations in perspective and allow them an opportunity to speculate, with a sympathetic and encouraging mentor, on strategies for improving areas which they conclude are legitimately of concern.

In the same way that the preservice survey is designed to encourage teaching assistants to consider specific aspects of teaching, the items on the student-evaluation questionnaire are intended to encourage them to think about what a good writing course and good pedagogy are. And like the preservice survey, the items on the student evaluation form are consciousness-raising. Planning, revising, and editing are all included as positive activities. Items addressing the instructor's availability to students outside of class and preparation for

---

[3]The computer form on which students complete the evaluation also has a space on the reverse for comments. Teaching assistants receive both a printout summarizing their own ratings and giving the mean score for each item and the original forms with the comments.

conducting class similarly imply program values. Thus when teaching assistants select items for their evaluations, they have the opportunity, encouraged by their mentors, to consider how well they anticipate doing on specific items, to think about the items they are reluctant to include and the reason for that reluctance, and to determine, even before they see the results, whether there are aspects of their teaching they want to revise.

TEACHING PORTFOLIOS

Teaching portfolios are becoming a familiar supplement to and in some cases a replacement for more conventional means of evaluating teachers at all levels, from elementary school through university. Although compiling and evaluating teaching portfolios can be time-consuming, as Wolf (1991) pointed out, portfolios provide a number of benefits that are not easily achieved through other means of assessment, such as observations and student evaluations. In particular he explained, "Portfolios enable teachers to document their teaching in an authentic setting and to bring in the context of their own classrooms in a way that no other form of assessment can," because unlike classroom observations:

> Through portfolios, teaching and learning can be seen as they unfold and extend over time. And when the actual artifacts of teaching are combined with a teacher's reflections, portfolios permit us to look beneath the surface of the performance itself and examine the decisions that shaped a teacher's actions. (p. 136)

The advantages Wolf discussed have been supported and elaborated on by others, and specific suggestions for using portfolios to evaluate teachers appear in recent work by Anson (1994), Edgerton, Hutchings, and Quinlan (1991), and Seldin (1991). Anson in particular focused on the importance of what he called "secondary documents" in teaching portfolios, including "reflections on peer-observations or videotapes, reflections on course evaluations, self-evaluations . . . [and] narrative accounts of problem-solving," which, he explained, supplement the "primary documents [which] are actual materials from classroom instruction." The "secondary documents . . . demonstrate active, critical thinking about instructional issues and materials" (p. 187).

Such secondary documents are at the heart of a portfolio's value in promoting self-assessment. They are explicitly reflective and evaluative, demanding that teachers consciously consider their motives for teaching in a certain way, for choosing specific materials, for responding to student work as they have, and so on. They require a teacher to consider what worked and what didn't and why, and they provide an opportunity to plan to revise those strategies, assignments, and materials with which she is dissatisfied. The inclusion of secondary documents is one of the distinguishing features between a teaching portfolio and a teaching file or resume, which are typically only collections of material.

A second distinguishing feature of the teaching portfolio is that it is a selected collection of teaching materials, and the selection process itself provides another kind of opportunity for self-reflection and self-assessment. In some cases, the contents of the portfolio may be specified by those requiring or conducting the evaluation of teaching: a state agency, a school system administration, a department or writing program. In other instances, the teachers being evaluated select what they will include in their portfolios. Sometimes the selection decisions are made by individual teachers, sometimes by teachers collaborating with one another. Most frequently, however, what appears in a portfolio is a mixture of required material, some of it common to all those making portfolios, and some of it specific to the individual teacher. For example, in our program, teaching assistants must provide certain common information: a teaching history that outlines which courses they have taught, an evaluation by a course director or delegate, and three sample evaluated student papers representing a range of student abilities, accompanied by the assignment for the paper. Within this set of required material, teaching assistants obviously have the opportunity to select the assignment(s) and student papers they include in the portfolio. An additional required item is an evaluation, but here the teachers have an option of including summaries of student evaluations and reflections on them or self-evaluations. The former option is typically chosen by classroom teachers, but some of our instructors have nonclassroom assignments, as program assistants, Writing Lab tutors, computer lab liaisons, or raters for the university's writing proficiency office. This group of teaching assistants often write self-assessments in which they explain their responsibilities, what they have learned from them, and how they feel they have benefited those they serve. In addition to the required material, teaching assistants may include, and most do, up to five pieces of additional material that they feel demonstrates the nature and quality of their teaching. This optional material usually includes original assignments or classroom materials, syllabi for new courses, and so on. Obviously, teachers have the freedom to select these materials and to explain them in a way that the teachers feel best reflects their purpose and usefulness.

One selection decision that teachers compiling portfolios may find themselves making is whether the portfolio should represent only the best aspects of their teaching or should also document efforts that failed, but from which the teacher learned. The fact that summaries of student evaluations are a required component of most teaching portfolios implies that the portfolio may include information that is not always flattering to the teacher. That is one reason we ask teachers to comment on these evaluations. We want them to have an opportunity to reflect on what students perceived to be successful as well as what they did not like, and often in these reflections, teachers are quite insightful about why something they tried did not work and how they will try to revise it—or why they will abandon it. Such reflection can be and I believe should be the center of the teaching portfolio. If teaching portfolios are seen as part of professional development, not simply as a way to evaluate teachers, then including and reflecting on some aspects of teaching that the teacher was dissatisfied with can be valuable and appropriate. However, this is obviously risky business for teachers. They must not only be told, but must believe, that explaining why an assignment or lesson bombed and what they learned from that experience will not be held against them. If teachers are to feel safe including anything other than what they consider exemplary work in their portfolios, the portfolio has to be presented within the context of a preparation or development program which assumes that all teachers both succeed and fail and that good teachers are those who reflect on and learn from both experiences. Those responsible for assessing portfolios must also be reminded of this, so that their assessment is supportive rather than punitive. In practice, what this means is that the instructor's reflections or self-assessments of both successes and failures must be considered as indications of good teaching.

CONCLUSION: SELF-ASSESSMENT, REFLECTION, AND TIME

The four strategies for encouraging new teachers to become reflective practitioners discussed in this chapter certainly are not the only approaches writing program administrators or others who prepare new teachers of writing might use. New teachers could be encouraged or required to write lesson plans for each class and to reflect in a teaching log on how those plans worked. They might be asked to keep a teaching journal in which they regularly write about their teaching experience or to visit one another's classes, write about what they observe, and meet to discuss these observations. Each of these strategies could be substituted for or used in conjunction with the four discussed earlier. However, it is important to remember that genuine and genuinely helpful self-assessment is time-consuming and that teachers, especially graduate teaching assistants, rarely have lots of extra time. If self-assessment is to help both teaching assistants and those who prepare and supervise them, its value must be clear and the time required for it must be reasonable. Otherwise, teachers may resent the time they must spend on it or treat it as busy work to be completed as quickly and effortlessly as possible. Despite their potential value, teaching logs and journals and visits to others' classes make large demands on people's time. Such is not the case of at least the first three strategies I have discussed here. Together, they are likely to take no more than an hour or two, and the preorientation survey is completed before teaching assistants even arrive on campus. The teaching portfolio, on the other hand, is time-consuming even when the materials which make them up are generated as a normal part of teaching. As Wolf (1991) and others have pointed out, selecting materials, writing the reflections, and composing the portfolio can place large demands on a teacher's time, and I would certainly caution against using portfolios in conjunction with another time-consuming reflective method. However, portfolios have, I believe, several advantages over journals or logs. First, their basic contents are drawn from the ordinary materials of teaching—from assignments, student work, syllabi, evaluations, and so on which teachers have easy access to. Teachers do have to "compose" the contents of their portfolios by selecting them, but they do not have to create them especially for the portfolio, and the selection process itself is, as I have mentioned earlier, a reflective process. Second, the teaching portfolio, as a collection of classroom material, has generative possibilities. That is, the teacher reviewing and selecting and reflecting on portfolio materials, either alone or in collaboration with peers, has the opportunity to discover concrete ways to revise her practices—to change an assignment, to revise a syllabus, to try another approach to responding to student writing. Finally, the teaching portfolio may help the new teaching assistant develop a professional resource, helpful later during a job search or useful as a model of what a tenure or promotion file might contain. Thus the teaching portfolio, particularly if it continues to gain acceptance in higher education, may have both immediate and continuing benefits for the teacher that makes the time required to compose it particularly well spent.

As Wood (1992) pointed out, teachers "need opportunities to raise, study, and interpret their own experiences and insights if they are to improve their practices" (p. 537). Although Wood wrote primarily about the advantages of such reflective practice for experienced teachers, I believe her point certainly applies to new teachers as well.

Critical self-reflection enables teachers to explore who they are and what they do in the classroom, and for new teaching assistants, such self-reflection can be particularly helpful in exploring the various subject positions they assume: They are students and they are teachers; they are at once novices and authorities, learners and possessors of knowledge. With support and guidance, new teaching assistants can be encouraged to examine these positions and the practices they imply, and in doing so to begin the continuing process of development as teachers.

REFERENCES

Anson, C. M. (1994). Portfolios for teachers: Writing our way to reflective practice. In L. Black, D. A. Daiker, J. Sommers, & G. Stygall (Eds.), *New directions in portfolio assessment* (pp. 185–200). Portsmouth, NH: Boynton/Cook Heinemann.

Braskamp, L. A., Brandenbury, D. C., & Ory, J. C. (1984). *Evaluating teaching effectiveness: A practical guide*. Beverly Hills, CA: Sage.

Edgerton, R., Hutchings, P., & Quinlan, K. (1991). *The teaching portfolio: Capturing the scholarship in teaching*. Washington, DC: American Association for Higher Education.

Schön, D. A. (1987). *Educating the reflective practitioner: Toward a new design for teaching and learning in the professions*. San Francisco: Jossey-Bass.

Seldin, P. (1980). *Successful faculty evaluation programs*. Crugers, NY: Coventry.

Seldin, P. (1991). *The teaching portfolio: A practical guide to improved performance and promotion tenure decisions*. Bolton, MA: Anker.

Weimer, M. (1990). *Improving college teaching: Strategies for developing instructional effectiveness*. San Francisco: Jossey-Bass.

Weiser, I. (1990). Surveying new teaching assistants: Who they are, what they know, and what they want to know. *WPA: Writing Program Administration, 14*(1-2), 63-71.

Wolf, K. (1991, October). The schoolteacher's portfolio: Issues in design, implementation, and evaluation. *Phi Delta Kappan*, 129-136.

Wood, D. R. (1992). Teaching narratives: A source for faculty development and evaluation. *Harvard Educational Review, 62*(4), 535-550.

Yancey, K. B. (1994) Make haste slowly: Graduate teaching assistants and portfolios. In L. Black, D. A. Daiker, J. Sommers, & G. Stygall (Eds.), *New directions in portfolio assessment* (pp. 210–218). Portsmouth, NH: Boynton/Cook Heinemann.

APPENDIX A

By taking a few minutes to answer the following questions, you can help tailor this year's orientation program for new teaching assistants to your concerns and interests.

PART I: Background and Experience

1.   Have you taught composition previously?
        Yes_____   No_____

2.   If your answer to 1 is yes, how many composition courses have you taught?
        1-3_____   4-6_____   7-10_____
        Over 10_____

3.   Have you had other kinds of college teaching experience? If so, specify the kinds of teaching you have done.

4.   Have you had elementary, middle, or high school teaching experience?
        Yes_____   No_____

5.   Have you had any formal (i.e., classes) or informal (i.e., workshops, in-service programs) training in teaching writing?
        Yes_____   No_____

        If you answer yes, please describe your training briefly. Use the back of this page if you need more space.

6.   Have you taken an introductory composition course yourself?
        Yes_____   No_____

        If you answer yes, please describe briefly the course (length of course, approximate number of papers, required reading, etc.). Use the back of this page if you wish.

        If you answer no, but such a course was generally required, did you test out, were you exempted, or did you fulfill the requirement in some other way (by taking a more advanced course, for example)?

7.   Which best describes the type of undergraduate school you
         attended?

         _____American publicly supported, over 10,000 students
         _____American publicly supported, under 10,000 students
         _____American privately supported, over 10,000 students
         _____American privately supported, under 10,000 students
         _____College or university not in United States

PART II: Subjects of Interest to You

Please indicate your interest in discussing and learning about each of the
following by numerically ranking the items in each group. Use 1 to
indicate the item most important to you in each group, 2 for the next
most important, and so on.

Group 1 (Rank 1-5)

         _____ What to say and do on the first day of class
         _____ Becoming familiar with the syllabus and text
         _____ Establishing class policies governing attendance,
               assignment deadlines, grading, office hours, etc.
         _____ Making an initial evaluation of your students' writing
               skills
         _____ Understanding the theory which underlies the course

Group 2 (Rank 1-6)

         _____ Making writing assignments
         _____ Commenting on students' papers
         _____ Grading students' papers
         _____ Identifying errors in grammar and mechanics
         _____ Using class time productively
         _____ Identifying students who need extra help (and knowing
               where they can get it)

Group 3 (Rank 1-5)

         _____ Helping students plan their writing
         _____ Helping students write for different audiences

_____ Helping students organize their writing

_____ Helping students respond to each others' writing

_____ Talking with students about their writing

Group 4 (Rank 1-5)

_____ Departmental procedures for evaluating and rewarding your teaching

_____ Your status as a student/employee (fees, benefits, etc.)

_____ Computing facilities available to you

_____ Other writing courses offered by the English Department

_____ Other opportunities for teaching in the English Department

Please feel free to use the back of this questionnaire for any comments you wish to make about matters of concern to you as a new teaching assistant at Purdue. Use the enclosed envelope to return the questionnaire to me. I look forward to seeing you at our first orientation meeting. I'm sure that your responses here will help us make it valuable to you.

APPENDIX B

Mid-Semester Self- and Course-Evaluation

Midterm seems like a good time to reflect on how the semester has been going, where we'd like to see it go, and how it can get there. I'd like you to take a little time to respond to the following questions as a way of helping you think about your teaching so far and helping me think about ways to make the practicum serve your interests and needs. Please return this to me following October break. And if you need more space, would rather write on computer, etc., that's fine.

1.   What have you enjoyed most about teaching so far this semester?

2.   What surprised you most about teaching (or teaching writing) so far?

3.   What has been most frustrating to this point about teaching?

4.   What are you happiest with about your teaching—that is, what
        do you perceive your strengths as a teacher thus far to be? Are
        there ways you can build upon those strengths?

5.   What aspect of your teaching thus far are you most interested in
        improving—what are you least satisfied with? Do you have
        ideas about what you'll do to improve?

6.   What aspect of *the course* you are teaching are you most
        satisfied with?

7.   What aspect of *the course* are you least satisfied with? Do you
        have suggestions for ways to change this? Ideas for how you
        might change things next time around?

8.   Are there specific activities, topics of discussion, materials, etc.
        in the practicum that have been of most help so far this
        semester? What have they been?

9.   Are there specific activities, topics of discussion, materials, etc.
        that the practicum *could* provide which would help you in your
        teaching this semester? What would you suggest?

APPENDIX C

Purdue University Composition Program Instructor Evaluation Items

1.   This course helped me become a better writer
2.   This course helped me plan my writing
3.   This course helped me state a main idea (thesis, focus)
4.   This course helped me support a main idea (thesis, focus)
5.   This course helped me organize my ideas and information
6.   This course helped me adjust my writing to the needs of readers

7. This course helped me adjust my word choice to my writing purpose
8. This course helped me adjust my sentences to my writing purpose
9. This course helped me revise my papers
10. This course helped me edit my papers to correct errors
11. This course helped me analyze my own and other students' writing
12. This course helped me clarify my ideas through writing
13. This course helped me write in other courses
14. This course helped me develop a research question or problem
15. This course helped me find information in the library
16. This course helped me evaluate what I read
17. This course helped me synthesize information from several sources
18. This course helped me support a main idea through research
19. This course helped me document sources
20. My teacher regularly prepares for class
21. My teacher presents information clearly and effectively
22. My teacher encourages questions and class discussions
23. My teacher relates reading assignments to writing assignments
24. My teacher uses class time productively
25. My teacher encourages group work for writing
26. My teacher relates assignments to the goals of the course
27. My teacher explains the purpose of writing assignments
28. My teacher explains the standards for grading
29. My teacher returns most assignments within a week
30. Comments on my papers help me improve my writing
31. My teacher encourages students to use the Writing Lab
32. My teacher is available to confer outside of class
33. Conferences with my teacher have been valuable to me
34. My teacher responds to questions with consideration
35. My teacher is interested in me as a person as well as a student
36. My teacher is friendly and accessible
37. My teacher explains policies for attendance and late assignments
38. My teacher shows cultural awareness and sensitivity to students
39. This course helped me understand the nature of group work
40. This course helped me develop my visual thinking abilities
41. This course helped me better understand problem solving
42. This course helped me better understand document design
43. Interacting with other students in my class helped me learn
44. This course helped me understand society and culture in new ways

45.   This course helped me understand academic experiences in new
        ways
46.   This course helped me understand ways audiences affect my
        writing
47.   This course helped me understand material in other courses
48.   Assigned readings helped me write my own papers
49.   Assigned readings helped me understand concepts discussed in
        class
50.   This course helped me read and evaluate texts critically
51.   I understand the methods of evaluation used to grade my work
52.   Methods of evaluation used to grade my work are fair
53.   My instructor treats students with respect
901.   My instructor motivates me to do my best work
902.   My instructor explains difficult material clearly
903.   Course assignments are interesting and stimulating
904.   Overall, this course is among the best I have ever taken
905.   Overall, this instructor is among the best teachers I have known

10 NEGOTIATING TA CULTURE

Sandra Mano

University of California, Los Angeles

I have always prided myself on being a concerned, nurturing teacher who facilitated learning in my classroom through a liberatory classroom pedagogy based on models proposed by Paolo Freire, Ira Schor, or Henry Giroux. I like to believe that my classes are student-centered, that I am empowering my students to take control of their own learning, and that I am sharing power in the classroom. I also teach my students to stress the rhetorical principles of audience and purpose. Yet when I became the Coordinator of TA Training in an English Department at a large research university, I found myself not paying sufficient attention to these principles, with serious consequences.

Part of the problem resulted from a clash of cultures in the contact zone, to borrow Mary Louise Pratt's phrase (Pratt, 1991). I had not recognized that I was negotiating between different cultures with different values: the English Department, their graduate students, and Writing Programs, of which I was a member. Another complication occurred because I saw myself possessing knowledge my students would be eager to have without fully understanding the power relationships involved. As an untenured lecturer from a writing program, I had no real authority over English graduate students. The students, feeling exploited within their department, saw me as trying to usurp power for Writing Programs that was not legitimately ours. I forgot that even a liberatory pedagogy still relies, although unconsciously, on the authority of the institution, the power of the grade, and our students' tacit acknowledgment of our expertise. My own unconscious reliance on that unspoken contract between student and teacher was exposed when I took over the position of Coordinator of TA Training. In addition, I had to confront my unwillingness to institute a truly student-centered curriculum in a situation when I saw my role more as a "trainer" than as a facilitator. On my part, these decisions were largely made on an unconscious level. They might have gone unnoticed expect for the set of circumstances I describe in this chapter. As it was, they were bad miscalculations. Although none of these mistakes are disastrous, they do reveal some of the problems we can get into as teachers when we misread our audiences and when we neglect, perhaps for good motives, the principles on which we base our teaching. In order to fulfill my goals as an instructor, I had to recognize several things about the situation and my teaching that were painful realizations. This chapter reports the difficult process of self-assessment I went through in order to maximize the effectiveness of my teacher preparation classes. To clarify the context, I begin by explaining the circumstances of the position and the relationship between the English Department and the Writing Programs.

SETTING THE SCENE

Writing Programs is a semi-independent program composed entirely of full-time lecturers, who have one year renewable contracts for the first 6 years and then after a major review, are hired on 3-year renewable contracts. The program has strong connections to the English Department. The English Department Executive Committee must approve Writing Programs appointments, and the Director of our program sits on their Executive Committee. For many years, that director was a tenured English Department faculty member but is now a Writing Programs Lecturer. However, the two departments are housed in separate buildings, and there is minimal contact between faculties. Yet, the Coordinator of TA Training appointment is filled by Writing Programs personnel. That person then moves to an office in the English Department and, although still a Writing Programs Lecturer, for all practical purposes works in and for the English Department. Our situation is not atypical: Writing Programs faculty are nontenured and because of their specialization in composition are not regarded as full-fledged colleagues by English Department faculty. A Writing Programs faculty member serves as the Coordinator of TA Training and all TAs are English Department graduate students. Like many other administrators across the country who are nontenured faculty put in charge of graduate students, the coordinator finds herself wanting to change practice, but without the authority to do so.

For these reasons, the position often had been hard to fill. Nevertheless, from the day I was hired as a lecturer, I was interested in the job. After all, I had just completed a prestigious PhD program in Rhetoric, Language, and Literature. I had studied linguistics, current theory, and pedagogy and was anxious to share new theoretical and practical insights. In addition, I had many years of classroom composition teaching experience. Although other lecturers who had served as the Coordinator complained about the position, I was eager to have a hand in TA preparation. I couldn't wait to share my theoretical and practical perspectives with new teachers. My enthusiasm and my belief in my "professional expertise" led me to underestimate the difficulties of the position and to forget some basic principles of liberatory education that I usually incorporated in my teaching. I had also forgotten the maxim of popular psychology which cautions that change can only be effected gradually by baby steps. Finally, after 6 years in the program, and fresh from the pleasant experience of having created a mentor program pairing our experienced composition faculty with new TAs, I was appointed Coordinator of TA Training.

CUT OFF AT THE PASS

My tenure in the office did not begin auspiciously. The culture of the English Department is based on a hierarchy that values faculty over staff. In spite of the fact that I was a faculty member in Writing Programs and would be teaching the teacher preparation courses, because I was situated and was often working with staff, I was considered a staff member by the English Department. One of the first messages I received on my answering machine addressed me by my first name, but the caller referred to herself as professor. This trifling incident pointed to one of the problems within the position and foreshadowed later encounters in my classroom: English graduate students, who might be said to comprise their own cultural group, are situated far down the hierarchy within the department. They were very conscious of distinctions between faculty and staff. Because I really wasn't considered a colleague by the English faculty, nor as someone whose research was of interest to an English department, the graduate students also discounted my expertise. This attitude shaped their responses to me in my teacher preparation class.

My position was further undermined by my lack of power to hire or fire TAs. TAs are chosen by the TA selection committee in the English Department and as long as they are making satisfactory grades and progress toward their degrees, they can teach. Writing Programs has no power to veto appointments. TAs, like most graduate students, are overcommitted and those teaching for the first time are also taking two courses on the quarter system. The teacher training courses, which do not directly bear on their careers and are not taught by a faculty member who will have influence over exams, dissertation, and so forth, are, not surprisingly, very low on their list of priorities. Very few even ask for letters of recommendation from Writing Programs personnel. In fact, some graduate students believe that too much emphasis on composition teaching will adversely effect their opportunity for a career in literature.

Another example of my powerlessness concerned grading the teacher preparation courses. These two unit, two quarters of instruction are graded satisfactory and unsatisfactory, although an unspoken English Department directive mandated that everyone receive a "satisfactory." TAs in theory are required to attend the class, but there is no practical way to enforce attendance or to insist that they do any reading or other work because the English Department has refused to allow Writing Programs faculty to grade their graduate students.

Although TAs teach first-year writing courses offered by Writing Programs, we have only minimal control over their curriculum. TAs design their own syllabi, choose their own texts, and create their own assignments. We distribute sample syllabi and guidelines to the course recommending the number and type of papers required, and a list of recommended texts (mostly readers). However, these are only recommendations. We don't have the power to mandate that they follow any of our procedures. Many do follow our suggestions, but TAs who wish to deviate from these patterns can and do. I tried to convince a TA not to select a text that our program had deemed inappropriate, but she complained to her faculty advisor who told her she was the final authority.

One of the difficulties in influencing TAs results from their own sense of expertise as readers and writers. After all, as English graduate students they feel like experts in anything relating to English literacy. Because the Coordinator of TA Training and the other mentors lack the authority of English Department faculty, we can't exercise much control over what TAs do in their own classrooms.

We also find little sympathy for our complaints or for mandating certain curricular and pedagogical practices among English Department faculty. They were familiar with a model where TAs were handed a text and a syllabus and sent into the classroom with no other preparation. Successful teaching was often not only undervalued but seen as risky. Several faculty warn students not to spend too much time on their teaching because that might interfere with their own work—one recipient of the yearly award for excellence in teaching was even told by his advisor that it wouldn't look good on his record to have future employers think he spent too much time on his teaching! He was cautioned that they might think he wouldn't spend enough time on research and writing.

When I began my new job, I was naively unaware of many of these complexities. I also did not fully understand that, for the TAs, those of us who were working in composition as full-time lecturers were losers who had not made it in literature. For most of them, it was incomprehensible that a professional might want a career teaching and researching composition or that our jobs might have some advantages over some tenure-track positions: teaching load, location, salary. I didn't realize that for the graduate students I was the "other," whereas I had assumed that we were as one. In addition, I represented a culture that held very different values from the culture of the English Department or the culture of the graduate students. Teaching—especially teaching writing to undergraduates—was high on my priority list. Because TAs taught so many of the first-year English sections, TA development was thus the cornerstone to improving undergraduate writing instruction.

However, I too, in my zeal to share what I had learned, made some costly miscalculations. Because of the scope of the material I had to cover in very limited contact hours, and my enthusiasm in sharing what I thought of as worthwhile information, I ignored the principles on which I usually base my classes: input from students on all aspects of the curriculum. My assumptions that the TAs and I shared certain cultural values that would allow me to take shortcuts led to resistance and rebellion on their part and painful reevaluation on mine.

REALITY BITES

In spite of an inauspicious beginning, I entered my class full of enthusiasm. I found that attendance was generally good and the TAs seemed to react favorably to my suggestions. They were willing to share experiences and talk about assignments and responding to student writing. Where I ran into difficulties with some TAs was in the area of theory. Graduate students in English often come to teaching with little personal experience as students in writing classes. Many placed out of their own first-year English classes. Few think of themselves as having writing problems, so they find it difficult to relate to students who feel insecure as writers. Others are so taken with their own newly acquired knowledge in the field of literature that they want their first-year students to write papers that are well beyond their capabilities at that stage. Much of this conflict is instantiated in the issue of the teaching of grammar and grammatical correctness because this is an area where English graduate students feel they can assert their authority. This conflict emerged when we began looking at student papers.

Although many were open to learning new theories of language acquisition and new approaches to teaching grammar, there was a vocal group of 5 in the class of 25 who violently disagreed with new approaches. When I presented evidence from research, they hardened their opposition and became openly hostile. Although they attended class, they usually scoffed at the points I made. I ended the quarter dreading the class and feeling very much a failure. In addition, when I visited the composition sections taught by my disgruntled students, I was dismayed to find that they were teaching literary explication rather than writing. Realizing that I was powerless to mandate a change in their classroom practice, I became even more discouraged. The students, however, were able to exercise their power by attacking me in the course evaluations (one gave me a 1 on a 9-point scale, seriously reducing my average score. Our scores are crucial because they are the basis on which our contracts are renewed.)

In a attempt to better understand the dynamics in my classroom and what was really at issue, I interviewed one of the mildly hostile students. He opened my eyes to the attitude of many of the others: "You shouldn't try to present yourself as an expert," he said. "When you presented research you really annoyed us. If you had said that you learned that from your teaching that would have been okay, but you shouldn't try to be an expert." His words forced me to acknowledge my awkward situation and the dilemma I faced. How could I reconcile my own sense of professionalism with this attitude? Was there a way to both feel good about myself and have a good relationship with the graduate students? Could I in good conscience alter what I believed I needed to do in the class in order to retain student good will and still teach conscientiously? How much of this situation was a function of the clash of cultures and particularly the hierarchy and working conditions of TA culture?

REEVALUATING AND LETTING GO

The realization that students would not accept my expertise was very painful. In fact, they might well resist my suggestions more vehemently if I called on that expertise. My opinions would not carry much authority. Even points of view commonly held in the profession had to be left open for discussion as though all options were equally viable. Acknowledging this mandated a change in my attitude.

Based on my professional preparation and teaching experience, I, of course, had many opinions about what our first-year students needed and what constituted effective teaching. I favored an approach that encouraged them to take risks, while giving them support and encouragement. However, such an approach was viewed as a sign of weakness by a percentage of the male students. Gender did seem to play a role in the rebellion because all the hostile students were male.

Moreover, our program, although giving the instructor a great deal of individual freedom to design a syllabus, does call for certain pedagogical approaches. We try to implement a process model, using revision, peer editing, collaborative learning. However, I had to let go of an attitude that took these approaches for granted and put myself in a frame of mind where I was willing to rehash these once more. For some TAs the insights gained from both research and lore in composition would always be challenged. What experienced composition professionals might consider as basic assumptions—for example, that it was not necessary or even helpful to mark every error on a paper, and that peer editing was a useful way to engage students in active learning—became topics for discussion and argument in class. Students challenged each piece of research. I am not suggesting that research should be accepted at face value or that it should not be questioned, but students were not willing to do the work necessary to effectively challenge the research—rather, their typical attitude was that if they didn't personally didn't like some activity, small group work, for example, then they shouldn't use it in their classroom. Their view of classroom practice is that it should serve institutions. They didn't really want to actively engage in the topics under discussion; they just wanted to discount the results and remain comfortable with their own ideas. I was never sure I effectively responded to these challenges, but I was aware that I had to take them seriously and not alienate students when they asked the most basic questions or when they questioned my suggestions. Pressuring TAs to accept my ideas or my methodology would only harden their resistance and would limit their willingness to use current research and practice in composition to inform their teaching. I had to be careful not to impose my cultural values, and I found myself couching most of my suggestions in a framework that began "I have found" or "some people believe but others question" and that concluded "you have to decide what works best for you—try out these methods and see what you feel comfortable using in the classroom and what your students respond to."

SHARING POWER AND RESPONSIBILITY

Self-assessment led directly to an adjustment of my classroom practice. I was used to sharing power with my freshman composition students and in fact often let them choose their readings, writing topics, and grading standards. I had to find a way to share power with the graduate students and allow them to take more control and responsibility for their own learning. One way was to try to engage the students in the debates that were going on in the field, much like Graff's (1992) idea of teaching the conflicts. Then we could discuss new research without my having to take an expert stance or to advocate a particular side of an issue.

I revised my syllabus to include current issues about which students might already have strong opinions (the necessity of teaching grammar, for example) and presented these as questions open for discussion and debate. A liberatory model based on student engagement would encourage them to read material on both sides of a question and even bring in their own sources.

One of the constraints in my situation was that students were so overburdened with their other work that I could only get them to read short pieces that I brought in. Most of them would come to class and participate in activities, but although many seemed to have good intentions to do outside work, their own schedules and the fact that we are on the quarter system made expecting much unrealistic. Although I had originally chosen two books and a packet of articles for them to read, I realized that I would be better off putting copies of the books on reserve and recommending readings rather than assigning them. I did insist that they buy the packet of articles (which I reduced to a minimum cost) and I even had some students who didn't want to pay the $15.00 cost of the packet. I assigned one or two articles weekly, but rather then assume that everyone would read them, I had students volunteer to take responsibility for the articles and present a short in-class summary. My hope was that when the other students heard a summary of the article, they would either be motivated to read it themselves, or at least would know that it was available as a reference when they began teaching. Most of the students were willing to sign up to present a reading, and for the most part, they were conscientious in fulfilling their commitments.

I also realized that if I wanted to establish communication between composition and TA culture, I had to be willing to proceed with the help of informants from the other group. I accomplished this by more actively involving the two TA peer consultants in designing the syllabus. This worked extremely well when the consultants were in tune with my thinking and less well when they come from a somewhat different approach. However, as much as possible, I tried to encourage them to coteach the class.

In order to further engage the graduate students in the intellectual discussions in the field, I brought in materials from conferences I attended during the year and tried to interest them in ongoing debates, such as the one about the role of first-year writing in the academy. In addition, I tried to get them to relate their own research interests to composition. When several members of the class were also enrolled in a seminar on feminist criticism, I urged them to investigate feminist approaches to composition studies. However, these tactics met with only limited success. Most of the students still compartmentalized composition and couldn't see how it could relate to the acquisition of knowledge in the field of literature. In addition, students who were not yet teaching often did not realize what they needed to learn until they were actually in the classroom, so they couldn't see the relevance of issues we discussed. It was painful for me to realize that what I valued so highly was peripheral for most of them, but it was crucial for me to understand their situation in order to most effectively reach this audience.

CHANGING PEDAGOGICAL STANCES

One of my frustrations when I observed TA-taught classes was their heavy reliance on teacher-led discussion. In this model, TAs asked questions and students were supposed to intuit the correct answers. Often these questions focused on the literary qualities of the text—not surprising coming from graduate students in a program that focused on literature and did not have a rhetoric or composition strand. I suppose I imagined that the new TAs might have absorbed our values from contact with their more experienced peers, but the TA culture has not adopted our value system; literature professors are still their teaching models. This is not to imply that these were always negative models or that there is only one way to effectively teach writing. In fact, I think that we have learned that there are many effective writing teachers and many effective methods. Nevertheless, many TAs used classroom strategies that I felt were not conducive to good teaching and learning. Should I observe these without objecting? Should I let these proceed unchallenged? If I seemed to be challenging students, I seemed to run the risk of alienating them to such an extent that they wouldn't listen to any of my suggestions. My alternative seemed to be to try to influence through example and to be satisfied with small amounts of change and cumulative progress through time. I had to face the reality that graduate students would be able to run their own classes pretty much as they wished and I had to think about more indirect ways I could influence them to adopt pedagogical tactics that would be effective in helping their students become better academic writers.

One strategy was to spend a lot of our class time trying to model desired activities in the training class, such as small group work, collaborative learning, peer editing. I also tried to get TAs to analyze their own writing processes and to remember their feelings as novice writers. Although they usually seemed to respond and be engaged in this activity, I'm not sure that it made them more sensitive to the difficulties their inexperienced students might be having with their assignments. My challenge was to remain patient as I responded to what would sometimes seem like frivolous challenges and objections.

Another method was to encourage them to visit classes taught by experienced TAs and lecturers. However, because time constraints and their own busy schedules interfered with this, I decided to cancel some of our class time and send them to observe first-year classes instead. I had to acknowledge that helping them have a first-hand experience with a freshman class seemed more likely to influence their teaching than listening to anything I might have to say. Self-assessment enabled me to accept what was in many ways a difficult and painful realization: I could not serve as a pedagogical model for many of the TAs. Ideas and practices would be better received from members of their own culture, and it was my job to expose them to peers who had accepted many of our practices. Trying to work against the TAs culture was counterproductive because it generated resistance. Recognizing its power and my own lack of power to effect instant change and working within the system was a more reasoned approach.

In order to put TAs in closer contact with experienced teachers, I invited TAs and mentors from Writing Programs to come to our class and share syllabi and assignments. TAs would have liked literature professors to come and share their pedagogical strategies, but the few I invited couldn't fit out class into their schedules. During the second quarter of the class, mentors joined us every other week and met with their mentees to discuss the week's discussion topic as well as teaching experiences. This seemed to work well because it served two purposes: It assured that the TAs would all be available to meet with their mentors at least once every other week, and it involved them in small group discussions in their mentor groups.

I wish that I could report that my changes met with unqualified success. That was not the case. I did improve my experience in the classroom and my evaluations. More importantly, I did see gradual improvement in teaching and learning when I visited TA classes. Over my 3-year tenure in the office, I saw more TAs using models in the classroom that I am convinced are more effective for teaching writing than the formulaic methods of old. There is more active learning and more collaboration. TAs, with the help of mentors who monitor their responses to student papers, make more sensitive and useful comments and are more sensitive to issues of ownership of texts. However, these changes fall short of my original goals. I realized that I had the naive idea that I could come in and institute major change. Again, my "hubris" led me to seriously misjudge my audience and the possibilities of my position. My biggest realization was how limited we are in our impact and in our ability to effect major change. I would have to be satisfied with small improvements, and that perhaps this was what one could most reasonably expect.

AND THEY DIDN'T LIVE HAPPILY EVER AFTER

In spite of my somewhat upbeat ending, this story is not in any way a tale of unqualified success. During my last year in the position I faced new challenges. One of my major goals in the training course was to help TAs meet the needs of our very diverse student body through a multiethnic approach; however, TAs began to express resistance to using multiethnic materials as a stimulus for writing. Vocal TAs expressed the desire that the training course be more of a "rap" session, focusing entirely on personal, anecdotal experience. They also wanted more time spent on training them to be TAs in large literature classes. At the same time, the administration in Writing Programs began to pressure me and the English Department to make the training course more theoretical. I was caught between TAs who were resisting multiethnic curriculum and theory, an English Department that was unaware of the contemporary composition theory, and a Writing Program that wanted TAs to be more theoretically grounded.

TA coordinators, like myself, are caught in the proverbial catch-22. Often we are nontenured or in our case, nontenurable faculty. We are in a somewhat hostile environment, working in an English Department that doesn't value our expertise, or that is unaware of current approaches to composition. This situation is frequently reflected in the attitude of the graduate students who give teaching composition a low priority. My lack of awareness of these problems led me to vastly overestimate my ability to influence TAs. Because I did not realize that we represented different cultural values, I badly misread TAs as an audience. This misjudgment caused problems for myself as well as for the program. However, once I recognized the cultural gulf between us, I was better able to communicate across that gulf.

     As representatives of Writing Programs, we may always be outsiders to English Department members, but in spite of that we must learn to communicate with them, to use what we can of their expertise and status to effect change within the system, and to be satisfied with gradual progress. After my somewhat painful experiences as an administrator, I am more aware of the limitations of my power to influence students and to enact change. However, I am also heartened by the influence I did have and the changes (although gradual and perhaps minimal) that I did effect; and as painful as my self-assessment was, I have to admit that it was a useful reminder of the importance of understanding context and audience, of reaching across cultures to build community.

REFERENCES

Graff, G. (1992). *Beyond the culture wars: How teaching the conflicts can revitalize American education.* New York: Norton.

Pratt, M.L. (1991). Arts of the contact zone. *Profession, 91,* 33-40.

11 REFLECTIONS ON SELF-ASSESSMENT

Kathleen Blake Yancey
Clemson University

Jane Bowman Smith
Winthrop University

When we began to think about self-assessment in terms of this volume, we weren't entirely certain as to where our reflections and research would lead us. We knew what was in the literature: the observations by Susan Miller, for instance, about how experienced writers do in fact evaluate their own writing, and the projection and retrospection that Sondra Perl described in her discussion of composing processes. However, much of the literature seemed dated, and more recent work, such as Jean MacGregor's, focused on pedagogical applications. We knew, of course, what we do in our own classrooms, our own methods for inviting students to look at and get to know and then critique their own work. Until we found ourselves immersed in this project, though, we didn't fully appreciate the potential that self-assessment has to offer—in its current versions as explained here, but also in its promise.

In fact, as we review these chapters, it's easy to conclude that self-assessment seems to be one of the best kept secrets of the field. An Anson and Hilgers both suggest, self-assessment has been a part of the composing and revising landscape for decades. But it's been largely overlooked, and we have to wonder why. Perhaps it's because self-assessment's roots lie in self-evaluation and self-grading, or because self-assessment is best known as teacher-generated questions at an endpoint of composing. This view, however, is too limited. Perhaps, as Hilgers and his colleagues suggest, it's because self-assessment, with its emphasis on the self, seems at odds with the social constructionism that has so dominated the field of composition studies. Perhaps, as Lauer

and Latta suggest, it's a function of the postmodernism through whose
lens the unified self seems but a naive construct. Perhaps, as Howard
maintains, it's the result of our being unable to use self-assessment for
programmatic purposes that would validate it. In sum, we discern a
vacuum here, a space for the self—even a postmodern self—within our
theories and models and practices of composing, a self that was
accounted for at one time, but that has increasingly disappeared.

As the chapters here attest, however, any account of composing
would need to account for the self in writing and for the role that self-
assessment plays in composing: hence the exigence for this volume. And
as these chapters also suggest, neither the concept nor the phrase self-
assessment posits a singular self writing in a garret. Rather, self-
assessment is here defined as the processes that allow a learner to know
his or her own work—both in process and product—and to critique it
such that the work can be enhanced. We argue that the process of self-
assessment is essential to learning; the intellectual life demands that we
think about our own thinking. It's a method for assigning both
responsibility and authority to a learner, and it can take several forms.
What we do in this final chapter, then, is attempt to bring some
contingent order to our collective discussions of self-assessment and to
raise questions that we hope others will think through with us.

DEFINITION OF SELF-ASSESSMENT

Self-assessment can refer (a) to the processes that a learner uses to
realize (in the sense of making real) and to enhance learning; (b) to an
assessment of one's text; and (c) to an assessment of a self-as_____, for
example, an evaluation of self-as-writer.

Frequently, when the term self-assessment is invoked, the
reference is to the student's process of *thinking about* what she or he is
doing while in the process of that doing; thus a writer might focus on
what specifically she does as she revises in order to understand and to
improve her own revising practices. In this sense of the term, self-
assessment might never become public: It is a private part of the
student's reflection and learning. Schön calls this kind of assessment
"reflection in action" and argues that the awareness of and inquiry into
one's intellectual processes will make the learning more felicitous—in
the sense of a process being less problematic or a text more accessible or
closer to a writer's intent as a result of being described and understood.

Self-assessment can also refer to a more general procedure, often
making use of heuristics, that helps students to establish a habit of
critical inquiry that is active rather than passive, to integrate the learning

into what is already known, and to project what more can or should be learned. The assumption here is that such intellectual work helps students become more independent learners. Such self-assessment can occur at any phase of the composing process and can remain private or become public—shared with the teacher or other students.

Self-assessment can mean yet another procedure: one through which a student can establish a dialogue with the teacher for any of several reasons—to provide a progress report, to provide information about what has or has not been learned, to solicit help, to allow for evaluation. As many writers know, this kind of self-assessing dialogue is very similar to that engaged in by collaborative writers and by writers with editors. However, self-assessment can also mean the evaluation of a text: the kind of task that students are often asked to accomplish, for instance, in a portfolio cover letter or in a companion piece (a memo or letter that comes with a primary text to a teacher that explains to the teacher what is working and why, what is not working and why).

Finally, as Watson tells us, self-assessment can be an assessment of oneself, a tally of what one does well and does less well, and it can also be highly situated, as in the following example. A student in a given class writes an engaging narrative, engaging because the images are strong but less effective than it might be because the voice is weak; she couldn't find her way into the text. Her next paper, an argument, is delivered in a strong but uninformed voice. In her self-assessment, the student generalizes that she is a moderate writer, more successful in some rhetorical situations than in others. This assessment of herself as writer, therefore, plausibly cuts in at least two ways. On the one hand, such assessment works toward a kind of identity that, as Brooke has shown, is key to writing. On the other hand, such assessment can discourage as much as, and perhaps more than, enhance. The potential danger of self-assessment is here revealed in two ways. The student's self-assessment, in being so "situated," has been generalized to *all* of her writing, and this judgment may be erroneous. She has also generalized her writing in another potentially harmful way by ignoring her strengths and failing to define her weaknesses as areas for future attention. She has simply "summed up" her writing in ways that might not lead to growth.

Of course, the notion of self, which is at the heart of any self-assessment enterprise, is itself problematic. For Larson, the self is rhetorically situated, and to the extent that this self is informed, the practice of writing is more felicitous. For others like Latta, Lauer, and Howard, however, it is not the self we are about, but *selves*—and even these are coded institutionally and culturally. Their advice: to locate self-assessment in a matrix that not only permits but encourages plurality.

THE NATURE OF SELF-ASSESSMENT

Precisely because meaning is context bound, and because all self-assessment is ultimately about meaning, self-assessment is collaborative, even that not shared with others. It is in part through diverse contexts and communities that the self is defined. Several contributors make the point that for any writing task, self-assessment is located in several social situations:

- The rhetorical situation of a paper.
- The situation of the class, including peers and teachers.
- The situation of a student's prior learning.
- The situation of what the student plans to do next.

Just as important, self-assessment is dialogic; its very nature demands that the self call on others to help in its development. The request for self-assessment, regardless of the definition we mean here, relies on a student distancing himself from the processes he is using, from the learning he is gaining, from the text he is writing, from himself as one with the text. Thus a shared identity of text and writer is disrupted. The information gained in this process—a result of a new perspective—can be useful to a teacher: It frames a text in a new way for her as well, allowing her to experience the student's perspective, to reflect on his practice, to reflect on the faculty member's own teaching practice, and to respond usefully—it is a very complex interaction.

In this process, students often achieve a fruitful distance: perhaps because they are looking at the process in a more holistic, less atomized way, even when the text isn't finished. Even weak students can find in the process, as we see in Collins' chapter, that their insights shift, from ones grounded in observations like "this paper is just an assignment" to something more specific, as they try to understand what they have on the page in order to talk about it. As Anson suggests, the need to communicate about communication can be doubly good. And just as important, such dialogue also alters the relationship between teacher and student: The teacher, as Larson puts it, is more editor, less grader, less other.

To begin that dialogue, writers focus on a first step: The writer must begin to *know* his or her own writing, and no matter what form that process takes, the important point is that this knowing begin. Without it, as Anson suggests, no "expertise" is possible, and expertise is what self-assessment is about—authority about processes, about texts, about the writer.

Who exercises what kind of authority, however, is still one of the the quandaries that we struggle with within the discipline, as the debates of Bartholomae and Elbow make clear, and within this text as well. For some, self-assessment seems little more than a kind of expressive absorption with the self—which may account, at least in part, for why it has received so little attention, particularly given the role that social constructionism has played in composition studies within the last decade. Another—and we think, more accurate—way of understanding self-assessment is to see it as a highly ideological act. Latta and Lauer are correct, we think, when they suggest that self-assessment can lead merely to a student's simply internalizing and then reproducing a given set of institutional or cultural values. This can be done deliberately and cynically by some students, but also innocently by others, out of a mistaken belief in the nature of learning. The hope for self-assessment, however, is that the student—perhaps even before becoming enculturated—goes beyond our standards to his or her own, talks back to us, and begins to negotiate the terms that will govern a text, in much the same way as did the writers here. One way of understanding how efficacious self-assessment is, then, is to understand to what extent it encourages this kind of communication, this kind of meaning making, this kind of rhetorically effective resistance to institutional textual values.

Of course, when we talk about these behaviors—about developing criteria and talking back and negotiating terms—we are talking about behaviors that cut across assignments, that cut across classes, that, we hope, begin to help students develop what is often called a habit of mind: a disciplined way of seeing the world and engaging with it and writing it. Engaging the world, however, does not always lead to happiness. The learning we associate with self-assessment may lead to a sense of power, and indeed, may lead to power itself, but such learning comes at a cost, as Collins and Mano make clear. Sometimes that cost is a part of the process; it's cost with a small c. Sometimes the knowledge and understanding produced by self-assessment is cost with a capital C. It can show us the gap between intention and effect, between goals and achievement, between the simplicity and elegance of vision and the complexities and messiness of practicality. Likewise, self-assessment can show us that certain changes are not possible, at least not now. Still, the invitation to engage in self-assessment is an invitation to knowledge, of self and of text, and to the action that is only made possible with this kind of knowledge.

IMPLEMENTATION AND QUESTIONS

The diversity of insights, methods, and pedagogies here suggests the kind of issues that we teachers must engage when we use self-assessment with other students and the questions that such consideration entail:

- Larson and Watson take two sides of one issue, with Watson being more focused on the tacit, on students' discerning the criteria within themselves and articulating those. For Watson, the value of self-assessment is the value innate in reflection itself. Larson argues that students need to develop textual criteria, and also focuses on self-assessment as an act of reading: How do we teach students to read their texts in order to revise? The purpose here seems to be to help students to work independently, although this is achieved through students' beginning to understand how to structure texts. Precisely because it is so difficult to imagine the reader, Larson says, students need to understand more general, predictable responses to text—as structure, diction, voice and so on. The questions now: How does this approach tap what we know about composing? How else might we use this approach in class?

- Anson's sense of intention contributes to our understanding of self-assessment as well. Like Larson, he suggests that students' skill in analyzing texts is underdeveloped. And like Larson, Anson is interested in the students' use of self-assessment—as a part of a composing repertoire (rather than to initiate a dialogue, for instance). But Anson reminds us of the role that a writer's intentions plays in any composing act; the fact that he asks students to discuss their intentions makes it more likely that they will have intentions. Such a request acts as a goal-setting device, and that seems to be an essential component to self-assessment as we're working with it. The question: What can students tell us about the role of intentions as they move from text to text? What role does such understanding have in the development of writers?

- We see a wide range of applications of self-assessment in the classroom, from Watson's "open letters" to Collins' specific, timed questions—the former being a request to reflect in a larger, more holistic way perhaps; the latter being a heuristic aimed at helping students complete a specific assignment. The kinds of self-assessments discussed in this collection have also dealt with both the process and the text. Is one kind of self-assessment assignment preferable to another, or is one perhaps better for a certain kind of intellectual task than another? Should teachers use several? What would be too much? (What are the limits of discipline here?)

- Given the ideological issue raised by Latta and Lauer, is it possible that self-assessment could serve as a bridge between and among multiple voices? How much "error," for instance, should we expect in students' self-assessment, and what exactly do we mean by error here? Don't students have to experiment, to make errors, in order to learn? Can a student's self-assessment be "wrong"? Are some students better at self-assessment than are others? Is the purpose of self-assessment just to "get it right"—as if only the teacher's view matters?

- How much, and in what form, should the teacher respond to self-assessments? These collected chapters suggest a continuum of possible strategies for teacher response. Hilgers and company include a sample of nonresponse, whereas Smith and Collins seem to suggest that quick and specific response is key to shaping behavior. And even if response is desirable, the nature of that response is another factor that raises questions. Both Smith and Mano remind us how easy it is for the teacher—in both responding and assigning—to take over students' self-assessments, to use them, with the best intentions, to serve the teacher's ends, rather than to let the students develop. How can self-assessments be used to help the student profit from the teacher's expertise but not to be smothered by it? Is it the case, then, that we must create a balance: the student's sense guided by or operative along with the teacher's? How can we encourage collaboration and negotiation among the student, text, and teacher through self-assessment?

- Both Collins and Watson also make the point that we need to examine our own practice and our assumptions—not just wait for the students to come up to our level. (And perhaps they will develop to another level that's quite different than ours.) We cannot forget our own authority and the power of both the institution and the grade, however. What role, if any, does self-assessment have in the grading process? How will we guard against the negative effects that grading can have on students?

- In another assessment context, Howard shows us a potential use beyond the individual student's and teacher's: to consult with students, to count on them to bring their own experience and their judgment about that experience to assist in making a programmatic decision about them. Are there other kinds of programmatic decisions that students can assist with, by means of self-assessment? And what goes into making such a decision? Do some students perform better than others in *this* task? How will we convince administrators and others to take the students' self-knowledge seriously?

- Weiser suggests how important self-assessment is to teachers as well. How might we help teachers who are already practicing in the field, and how else might we structure it into our teacher education programs?

CONCLUSION

In pondering this subject for some 6 years, first individually and then through the perspectives of our collaborators, we have realized both the complexity and flexibility of student self-assessment, and we hope we have suggested both its current worth and its future promise. Like Janus, self-assessment faces in two equally important directions: first, into the private world of the student's learning and her mind, as she reflects on her thought as well as her accomplishment. Second, it looks outward into the public world, as she assesses her work in any of several ways, negotiating—with her peers' and teacher's assistance—her individual desire for voice, content, and stance with the particular conventions governing her specific rhetorical context.

AUTHOR INDEX

A

Anson, C., 9, *20*, 146, *150*
Aristotle, 77, *95*
Aschbacher, P.R., 9, *22*
Atwell, N., 9, *20*

B

Badger, L., 9, *20*
Ball, S.J., 45, 50, *55*
Bandura, A., 108, 109, 118, *124*
Bayer, A., 9, 11, *22*
Bazerman, C., 39, *55*
Beach, R., 7, 9, 15, *20*, 36, *55*
Beaven, M.H., 15, *20*, 36, 44, *55*
Belanoff, P., 47, *56*, 107, 108, *124*
Belenky, M.F., 28, *32*
Bellack, A.S., 5, *20*
Berkenkotter, C., 63, *73*
Berlin, J.A., 8, *20*, 27, *32*, 39, 45, 46, 47, *47n*, *56*
Berthoff, A.E., 121, *124*, 125, 127, 137, *138*
Bissex, G., 7, *20*
Bizzell, P., 27, *32*
Black, J.L., 4, 5, *23*
Blanche, P., 19, *20*

Bolles, R.C., 108, *124*
Booth, W.C., *28n*, *95*
Bornstein, M.T., 4, *20*
Bornstein, P., 4, *20*
Bourdieu, P., 40, 41, 46, 49, 52, *56*
Brandenbury, D.C., 143, *150*
Brannon, L., 11, *22*
Braskamp, L.A., 143, *150*
Bridwell, L., 7, *20*
Brindley, G., 19, *20*
Brookfield, S.D., 128, 129, *138*
Bruffee, K., 8, 11, *20, 21*, 27, *32*
Bruner, J.S., 126, 127, 132, *138*
Bullock, R., 44, *56*
Burnham, C.C., 43, *56*
Butler, J., 28, *32*

C

Calkins, L.M., 9, *21*
Camp, R., 14, *21*
Carey, J., 46, *56*
Carey, L., 9, 14, 16, *21*
Carta, J.J., 4, *21*
Carter, K., 63, *73*
Cavior, N., 5, *21*
Cayton, M.K., 28, *32*
Chaffin, R., 28, *32*

SUBJECT INDEX

A

ability grouping (or tracking), 35, 44, 45, 46, 47, 50, 51
affective development, 25
agency, of learner, 26, 38-39, 41, 55, 87, 98, 109, 116, 118, 120, 157, 171-172
  as taking responsibility for writing, 107, 117, 121, 164, 170
argumentative essay, 16, 18, 94, 100, 171
assignments, teacher's working with, 12, 16, 52, 86-87, 122-123, 137, 147-148, 160-161, 166
  students' reactions to, 110, 113, 116, 121, 173
attitudes, students', 15-16, 48-50, 71, 76, 82, 85, 116, 142, 162
audience, concept of, 65, 71, 157
  as intended for a particular text, 12, 17, 60, 62, 97-98, 158
  students as audience for teacher, 165-168
  students imagining or creating, 16, 63, 68-69, 99, 111-113, 117, 141, 174

writer as reader of own text, 84, 100-101
authority of the teacher, 69, 94, 128, 141-142, 157-158, 160, 162, 168, 175
  student's deferring to, 69, 72, 98, 134, 137

B

Basic Writers, *See* writers, as beginners
blocks, writing, 28, 31, 106-107, 135
brain, hemispheres, 132

C

cognitive theory, 8, 38, 60
  cognitive growth, 15, 25
closure, intellectual, 130
coherence, 7, 18, 81
collaborative learning, 1, 11, 109, 141, 149, 163, 166-167, 172, 176
composing, acts of, 81-82, 88, 92, 101, 105
  models of, 7, 63, 170
  process, 5-6, 10, 17, 48, 63, 81, 105-106, 108, 117, 174